THE
PANZER SOLDIER

THE
PANZER SOLDIER

Wade Krawczyk

The Crowood Press

First published in 2006 by
The Crowood Press Ltd
Ramsbury, Marlborough
Wiltshire SN8 2HR

www.crowood.com

British Library Cataloguing-in-Publication Data
A catalogue record for this book is available from the British Library.

ISBN 1 86126 856 4
EAN 978 1 86126 856 3

Edited by Martin Windrow
Typeset by Jean Cussons Typesetting, Diss, Norfolk
Printed and bound by Craft Print International Ltd, Singapore

CONTENTS

PREFACE

That there has always been a significant interest in World War II is hardly surprising. Perhaps harder to explain is the specific interest in the armed forces of Germany, which certainly has nothing to do with any admiration for the political regime that they served. This curiosity appears to be generated by a recognition of the professionalism, technical and tactical expertise and daring demonstrated by many units of the Wehrmacht during the period 1939–45. Even the sternest critics of the Third Reich seldom refuse a respectful nod towards these high standards of training and performance. Among those who become interested in the practical aspects of the Wehrmacht's equipment, organization and record, some find themselves intrigued by the glamorous yet functional uniforms of the German armed services.

The greatest interest is inevitably attracted by what may be termed the military elites – the paratroops, Rommel's Afrikakorps, the U-boat crews and the Waffen-SS; and among these particularly visible elites the soldiers at the tip of the spear of *Blitzkrieg* warfare – the armoured *Panzertruppe* – have an undeniable place. Trading their horses for steel-clad horsepower in the pre-war years, the German armoured troops led the way in ushering in the new age of mobile warfare in 1939–40. Their early dominance of this new, modern battlefield seemed to be epitomized by their dramatic black uniforms and death's-head badges, inspired by the heritage of the Prussian hussars of Frederick the Great and Blücher. The uniforms of the armoured troops departed radically from the traditional field-grey of the German Army in both colour and cut; they were not only practically suited to their specific task, but retained the dashing glamour of the old cavalry.

The focus of this work is on the now-rare uniforms and other relics of the Armoured Troops of the German Army. Through detailed photographic examination it is possible to build an informative picture of what these men wore into combat, and from decorations and surviving documentation it is sometimes possible to trace their service on the battlefields of war-torn Europe. While several of the uniforms shown here might appear to be similar, close examination reveals many variations of detail which all further the reader's knowledge of the subject, and the examples illustrated include several extremely rare pieces. Period black-and-white photos can provide a great deal of useful information, but not as much as close-up colour photographs of surviving items. It is hoped that this approach will be found of benefit to collectors, modellers and costumiers, by enabling them to become familiar with the characteristic details of these uniforms.

Inevitably, most uniforms and associated items that survive in today's collections are from unknown sources; but at the centre of this work is a selection of grouped items named to identified individual soldiers. More than anonymous pieces of cloth, these groups offer us windows into a particular soldier's personal experience, through his uniforms, wartime photographs, documents and medals. These groups come from captured material, from the families of former soldiers, and even from the veterans themselves. As the men who fought in 1939–45 fade away, these are the artefacts of a now-vanishing era – the museum relics of the next age. For some it is all that remains of them, and these items echo their struggles and victories.

Wade Krawczyk
Brisbane
December 2005

Acknowledgements

As always there are many to thank, since it is impossible to produce a work such as this in isolation. The first person I must thank is my mother, Judith, who took me along to my first militaria auction back in 1975, thus creating the interest that endures to this day; this book is dedicated to her. I must also thank my patient wife Melissa and my little boy Max, who have both seen me through this task with support and cheer; this work is yours, too. I have enjoyed a great deal of support from friends in the field, but I would like to single out especially Peter von Lukacs and his family in Stockholm; Peter has been a best friend despite the distance, and a great support – thanks, my friend.

Sincere gratitude is also owed to the following, for access to items, for support and technical information: Dean Andrew, Mark Bakker, Maxime Blanc-Strauss, Peter Ekelund, Angel Farré, Scott Fielding, Mark Gibson, Bill Grist, Frank Heukemes, Michael Hidock, John Hodgin, Steve McAlpine, Duncan McLeod, Robert Noss, Scott Pritchett, Dale Ritter, Karen Savery, Mark Savery, Akira Takiguchi, Peter Walter, and Johan Van den Berge. I would also like to thank the following organizations: Hermann Historica of Munich, Germany, international auctioneers; and Military Antiques of Stockholm, Sweden (*www.military-antiques-stockholm.com*).

HEADGEAR
Panzer *Schutzmütze*

The Panzer *Schutzmütze* (literally, 'protection cap') first appeared with the introduction of the black vehicle uniform in 1934. It was designed to provide head protection while crewing and working with armoured vehicles, and consisted of a hard rubber helmet shaped like a skull cap, covered by a large beret in black wool.

* BeVo was the trademark of Bandfabrik Ewald Vorsteher of Wuppertal, a firm which produced high quality cloth insignia by a continuous band machine-weaving process.

The helmet portion was made of hard sponge rubber in a domed shape, which was then covered with black wool. The interior was lined with six wedge-shaped panels of black oilcloth, sewn together. Near the base of the seams were six pierced rubber ventilation eyelets; several were plugged with cork stoppers that could be removed or replaced to control ventilation. The sweatband was of a soft caramel-coloured kid leather, which was backed with a protective strip of rubberized cloth; under this was a soft buffer of white felt. A pronounced rim was apparent around the outside base of the helmet, to trap the edge of the beret when it was pulled over the helmet.

The large, Basque-style beret was made of woven wool, this method giving it a distinct spiral ribbed texture; at the top centre was a small tag where the weave started. The base or opening of the beret had an elastic quality that held it pressed into the groove at the base of the helmet.

At first the only badge applied was a white wreath embroidered directly into the beret with a metal cockade in the national colours of black, white and red pinned in the centre (**see photo, right**); however, in October 1935 the new German national emblem (the eagle and swastika) was added. The design changed to a flat 'BeVo'* machine-woven wreath and cockade, which was then hand-sewn to the beret, below a machine-woven national emblem.

While the *Schutzmütze* was innovative, its production and issue ceased in 1941. It was unpopular, and had become impractical with the increasing use of radio headphones by vehicle crews.

A version of this headgear was also produced for the artillery crews of Sturmgeschütz self-propelled assault guns (in effect, turretless tanks, deployed to support the infantry); this was identical apart from being produced in field-grey wool. The insignia were the same as on the black version, but machine-woven on dark green backing. This version was produced only in small numbers and is extremely rare today.

(Right) A very late production beret for the *Schutmütze*, dated 1940. The last pattern BeVo machine-woven insignia are in light grey; this colour was intended to provide a more subdued appearance in the field, but the idea was overtaken by the beret's withdrawal from service. Note that the late insignia are machine-sewn to the beret.

(Below) An extremely rare example of the insignia from the field-grey beret for Sturmgeschütz crews. The wreath and cockade are identical in design to the Panzer type, but on a dark green base. Interestingly, the eagle is in light grey, giving the same contrasting combination as in the period photograph **below right**. Note the ribbed weave of the field-grey wool berct, and the zig-zag machine stitching used to attach the badges to the beret.

(Right) The ribbed weave of the beret is also visible in this excellent photograph of the field-grey *Schutzmütze* for assault gun crews. Withdrawn from general issue at the same time as the black beret, it nevertheless saw some later use by personnel of motorized rocket batteries, as well as by crews of smaller armoured ammunition carrier vehicles, which often had no radio equipment, thus eliminating the headphone problem.

(**Left**) The interior of the beret is seen here with the segmented oilcloth lining, and a size stamp '55' on the sweatband. The woven cloth name labels of at least three major manufacturers may be found attached to the centre of the lining, but most examples lack these.

(**Right**) The exterior of the helmet was covered with black wool over the hard rubber body. Note the rubber ventilation eyelets, and the pronounced indent above the rim for holding the beret in place.

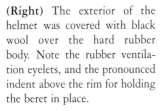

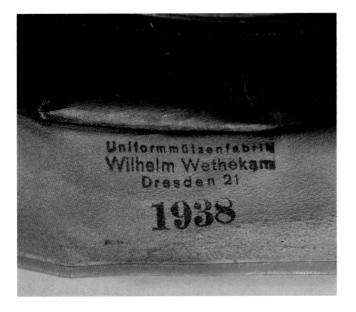

(**Left**) On the underside of the sweatband the stamp of the maker shows '*Uniformmützenfabrik* (uniform cap factory)/ *Wilhelm Wethekam/Dresden 21/ 1938*'. Most caps were ink-stamped by the manufacturer in this manner.

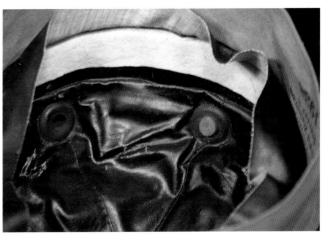

(**Right**) The rear of the sweatband is seen here, with its rubberized cloth backing strip and white felt buffer. Note also the stopper in the ventilation eyelet, provided to adjust airflow.

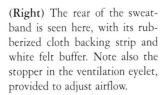

Black Panzer *Feldmütze* M1940 (enlisted ranks)

The black Panzer field cap was introduced in March 1940 to replace the *Schutzmütze* as the standard headgear for wear with the black uniform prescribed for use when serving with armoured vehicles. This change, as mentioned previously, was ordered because of the awkwardness of wearing the *Schutzmütze* in conjunction with the headphones of the radio equipment increasingly fitted to all vehicles; when the protective headgear was first designed, only a small minority of command vehicles were equipped with radios. In the period between the approval of the new black cap and its becoming generally available, armoured troops were often photographed wearing the general issue field-grey M1934 field cap with their black vehicle uniforms. During the 1940 Western campaign this was less often true of Panzer officers, who purchased their uniforms privately, and thus were able to obtain their silver-piped black version of the M1938 'new style officer's field cap' more quickly.

(**Left**) The cap was of exactly the same design as the M1934 field cap, but in black wool. Panzer troops wore a soutache of rose-pink *Waffenfarbe* – the identifying colour of their arm of service – surrounding the national cockade. The cockade and the national insignia may be found both on black base cloth, both on green, or on a combination of both as seen here. The cap shown was acquired in Moscow and is unissued, coming from Soviet-captured stocks. It carries both German stamps and Soviet capture markings.

(**Below**) The combination of black-backed and green-backed insignia is more clearly visible here. The soutache of rose-pink 'Russia braid' – an old military tailors' term for this doubled piping, and nothing to do with the Russian Front in World War II – is machine-sewn during construction of the cap, and the insignia are hand-sewn. Later some insignia were machine-sewn; and in mid-1942 the coloured Waffenfarbe soutache on all German field caps was ordered discontinued.

(**Left**) The convenience of the *Feldmütze* for personnel wearing radio headphones is clear in this wartime photograph.

(Left) This cap's lining is in a grey-brown brushed cotton. It displays the German markings on one side and the Soviet capture markings on the other. Here we see the stamp of the manufacturing group 'Lago – Berlin', which was a co-operative of smaller tailors. Below the word 'Jahr' is stamped '1941'; to the right of this are 'Große' (Large) and the size '55'. Below this is stamped 'B II 40', which is now believed to represent distribution from the second of two Berlin Heeresbekleidungsämpter (Army Clothing Depots) in 1940.

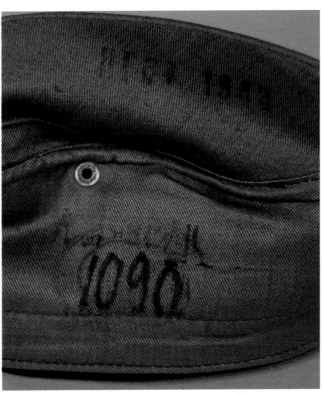

(Right) The other side displays the Soviet capture stamps and serial numbers; this piece was stamped in 1943. Note the second line of stitching near the base, a consistent feature of original caps; and the zinc ventilation eyelet with its split and splayed inner head over a backing washer.

(Left) A feature occasionally seen inside tunics and caps is the wool-manufacturer's identifying stamp, which was stencilled on the end of the huge bolts of fabric. Apparently this particular woollen mill was established as early as 1815.

Black Panzer Aufklärungs *Feldmütze* M1940 (enlisted ranks)

The black field cap was worn not only by tank crews, but also by other personnel who were required to wear the black vehicle uniform. Examples can be found with soutaches in red for the artillery, lemon-yellow for signals troops, copper-brown for some reconnaissance units (mid-1939 to early 1943, but rarely used), black-and-white twist for armoured engineers, on rare occasions in white for the Führer's Escort unit, and, as here, in golden-yellow for armoured reconnaissance (at first used specifically by former Kavallerie units converted to this role). Many soutaches show evidence of having been changed at unit level to one of a new Waffenfarbe rather than being factory-applied.

(**Left & below**) Machine-sewn to this cap during construction is the golden-yellow soutache worn by the Panzer Aufklärungs (armoured reconnaissance) troops, and by all members of 24. Panzer Division, which was converted to the armoured role from 1. Kavallerie Division at the end of 1941. Both insignia are those found on the general service field-grey sidecap: a grey-on-green eagle, and a cockade on dark green backing. The cockade has been machine-sewn, while the eagle is hand-sewn – such combinations are often encountered. Note also the small cable-stitches each side of the apex of the soutache to hold the front of the flap tight against the body. This was a common feature, which was later removed if the flap was turned down to cover the ears in cold weather.

(**Left**) The lining is in the usual soft grey-brown cotton twill. It bears the maker's stamp '*Willy/ Sprengpfeil/Mützenfabrik/ Hamburg 19*', the date '*1941*' and size '58'. Note the zinc ventilation eyelet with its split and splayed inner head and slightly domed washer.

Field-grey *Einheitsfeldmütze* M1943 (enlisted ranks)

Some regiments and divisions of the German Army had unofficial (but tolerated) or semi-official tradition badges. These might refer to the original region of recruitment, to the divisional sign as marked on vehicles and notice boards, or to some other motif of particular significance to that unit. On New Year's Eve 1944 an oakleaf tradition badge was officially approved for wear in all units of 1. Panzer Division by the divisional commander, the newly promoted Generalmajor Eberhard Thunert.

This badge, echoing the division's vehicle sign, had already been worn unofficially for some time by various troops of the division.

(**Right & below**) This cap, remarkably, was purchased directly from the garbage bag of a 'picker' in one of the 'flea markets' of Hamburg, Germany. Crushed flat from years of storage – note the prominent 'break' at the centre of the peak (visor) where it was folded – it had never before been in a collector's hands.

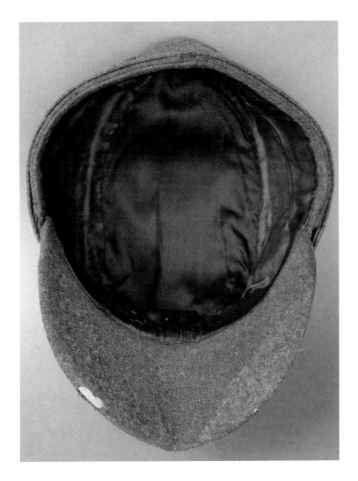

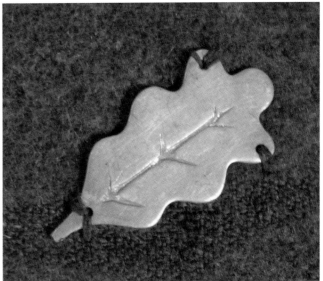

(**Above**) The cap is a completely standard field-grey M1943 *Einheitsfeldmütze* ('universal' or 'all arms' field cap), of the peaked design introduced in July 1943 and intended to replace the sidecap throughout the Army, Air Force, Waffen-SS and many other German uniformed organizations. (While its use became widespread by all ranks, complete replacement of the sidecap was never achieved, however.)

This piece has the subdued BeVo eagle and national cockade machine-woven into a field-grey backing of truncated triangular shape. The lining is made of silver-grey artificial silk; it is heavily grease-stained, and any original markings have been lost. Sewn at a slant to the left side is the oakleaf tradition badge of 1. Panzer Division. This is hand made from white sheet metal, with a central vein design engraved, and three sewing holes drilled through.

JACKETS
Black Panzer Aufklärungs *Panzerjacke*, first pattern (enlisted ranks)

The first pattern of the armoured vehicle service uniform – *Sonderbekleidung der Panzertruppe* ('special uniform of armoured troops') – was introduced in 1934 to accommodate the needs of the new Panzerwaffe. This practical and striking-looking uniform was to be unlike any before it, and in fact owed more to the fashionable ski clothing of the day than to any previous military uniform. The jacket featured a short waist, a deeply double-breasted front, and was without external pockets to snag on the many protrusions inside a tank. The colour black was chosen to hide oil stains, given the unavoidably dirty nature of the tank crewman's job, and because camouflage was hardly a consideration for soldiers who went into battle enclosed in armoured vehicles.

The first pattern was distinctive in that the deep lapels could not be fastened across, as was the case with subsequent models; no buttons to secure the left lapel across to the right breast were provided. The collar was also quite square-cut by comparison with later patterns. For all ranks the collar was piped all around, generally in rose-pink wool Waffenfarbe, although rare examples exist with golden-yellow piping for Aufklärungs units. The collar patches for all ranks were also black, of rhomboid shape and piped around the edges with wool Waffenfarbe. In the centre of each was a silver-finish metal *Totenkopf* or death's-head, a traditional badge recalling those worn on mirletons and fur colpacks by elite hussar regiments in the 18th and 19th centuries – the armoured branch readily identified with the historic traditions of the cavalry whose battlefield role they were taking over.

The first-pattern national emblem, machine-embroidered in white on a black wool backing, was sewn to the right breast. Rank was generally displayed on the shoulder straps alone (with the exception of the two senior privates' ranks of Gefreiter and Obergefreiter, which were identified by silver braid chevrons on the left sleeve only). The enlisted ranks' straps were originally completely sewn down to the shoulder of the tunic so as to prevent snagging, but after 1939 they were ordered unsewn, to allow for the use of slip-on cloth loops either concealing or displaying the unit designation.

The exceptional example of the *Panzerjacke* shown on pages 16–18 bears the distinctions of a member of the Panzer Aufklärungstruppe (armoured reconnaissance troops), who wore the black vehicle uniform when working in armoured cars and other light armoured vehicles. Before July 1938 these personnel wore the same rose-pink Waffenfarbe as tank troops, differenced by a Gothic 'A' cypher and the relevant unit number on the shoulder straps. It is constructed from very sturdy, high quality black wool; the German Army apparently believed that this fabric would offer some brief protection in the event of a fire. The lining is made from an early light grey cotton twill fabric. On the upper left interior there are the usual size markings, but in early large-size numerals. The manufacturer's name above these is '*G.Assmann Halle /S*' (for Saal), and below them is the depot stamp '*E35*' for Erfurt, 1935. Erfurt was home to 1. Panzer Brigade, which until October 1940 comprised Panzer Regimente 1 and 2, the tank component of 1. Panzer Division. A partially defaced label retains the identification of battalion headquarters, I Abteilung (battalion)/Panzer Regiment 1. When the original five Panzer divisions were first formed from 1935 onwards their main combat units included a tank brigade of two Panzer Regimente each with two battalions; a light infantry (Schützen) regiment with two battalions; an artillery regiment with two battalions, and a light reconnaissance battalion.

(**Left**) A portrait photograph dated 1939 shows a soldier of Aufkläungs Abteilung 3 wearing an almost identical jacket to that illustrated on pages 16–18. Note the Gothic 'A' above the battalion number on the shoulder straps. Note, too, the very pronounced overhang of the beret at the rear of the *Schutzmütze*.

(**Opposite**) Reconstruction: a Panzer soldier in 1939, wearing the *Schutzmütze* with a second-pattern *Panzerjacke* – note the buttons on the right breast for fastening the left lapel across for extra warmth. He carries an MG34 machine gun, the standard weapon mounted both internally and externally on German armoured fighting vehicles; this one is fitted with its shoulder stock and bipod, so comes from an external anti-aircraft/anti-personnel mounting rather than from the front hull or co-axial turret mounts.

(**Left**) Although now badged to the armoured reconnaissance battalion, this exceptionally rare jacket seems to have been the property at one time of a soldier of the HQ Company, 1st Bn, Panzer Regiment 1. The label (**below**) has the name inked out and later cut out, but '*Stab I./ Pz.-Rgt.1*' is still legible.

(**Right**) An interesting contemporary postcard emphasizes the lineage traced by the new armoured reconnaissance units from the old Imperial mounted regiments. It celebrates the ancestry of Aufklärungs Abteilung 4, based at Sonderhausen in Thuringia, in Dragoon Regiment No.15 (3rd Silesian). The black-uniformed armoured car NCO at right wears rose-pink Waffenfarbe piping. This Abteilung (literally, 'detachment', but used for battalion-sized units) provided the reconnaissance element of 1. Panzer Division.

(Right) Note the early, squarer collar shape, and the attractive deep rose-pink colour of the wool piping. The shape of the collar patch follows the edge of the collar exactly. This example has stamped aluminium death's-head badges with triangular nose sockets; early skulls can also be found in stamped brass and cast metal.

(Below) The rear of the collar shows the construction details.

The bold lines of zig-zag stitching hold in place the interfacing material that stiffens the collar. The backing fabric of the collar is left raw-cut in this early example; later unpiped collars were turned over and hemmed. Note the small reinforcing cable-stitch at the junction of the collar and lapel, a common early feature to prevent tearing at this vulnerable point; and the two round-section brass pins securing the *Totenkopf.*

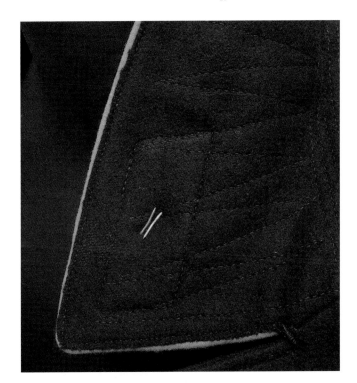

(Left) The early shoulder straps were a single, piped layer of cloth sewn directly to the shoulder all round; the securing stitches could be seen right through to the jacket lining. Arm-of-service cyphers such as this Gothic 'A' for 'Aufklärungs' were ordered to be removed from late 1939, but some troops simply sewed a patch of black cloth over the cyphers, so that they could be uncovered later. Here the battalion number below the cypher has been unpicked, but it appears to have been a '4'. The introduction in 1940 of slip-on loops bearing the cyphers saw the sewn-down straps replaced for a time with straps sewn into the shoulder seam at the outer end only; these later gave way in their turn to the more practical removable or 'slip-on' type, with an extra lower tongue passing through a 'bridle' loop at the point of the shoulder.

(Above) The national emblem was introduced for the *Panzerjacke* in November 1935, and many photographs prior to that date show soldiers wearing no emblems on either jacket or beret. The first pattern seen here was machine-embroidered in white on black wool, with very bold details.

(Right) The inner left side lining of the first-pattern jacket established the layout for all later models. It has a deep patch pocket with a crescent-shaped top and a vertical half-depth side opening; two small inner buttonhole tabs to engage the lower outside buttons on the right side; a vertical reinforcing strip beneath the armpit, supporting belt hook hangers; and a 'tunnel' for a waist adjustment tape, which was tied to give a snug fit. The manufacturer's and size markings (see text on page 14) are on the upper left, which is the most common but by no means the only place to find them. Just visible along the shoulder is the stitching for the sewn-down shoulder straps.

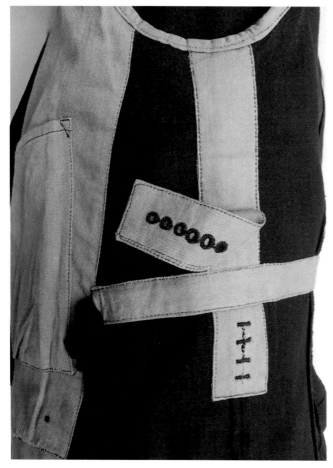

(Left) Lining of the inner right side; note the smaller, squared pocket with the opening at the top. Rolled back here for clarity is one of the cloth tapes suspended from the reinforcing strips beneath each arm showing the three alternative pairs of eyelets for fitting a wire suspension hook. The hook was punched through one of the three alternative slots in the waist of the jacket, between the four sets of horizontal stitching, and helped support the weight of the leather belt worn outside it. Note that the two upper slots here show signs of use. The waist adjustment tape and covering panel are also clearly visible; tapes came in black, grey or off-white.

Black Armoured Cavalry *Panzerjacke*, first pattern (enlisted ranks)

(Right) Seen here for the first time in print is the extremely rare first-pattern *Panzerjacke* piped in the golden-yellow Waffenfarbe for cavalry armoured car and other reconnaissance vehicle crews. In the 1930s most of the Kavallerie regiments were progressively mechanized, to perform essentially their traditional tasks – scouting ahead of large unit movements and screening their flanks and rear.

This tunic is marked inside to the Panzerspäh Lehr Schwadron (Armoured Scouting Instruction Squadron) of Kavallerie Lehr und Versuchs Abteilung 2 (Cavalry Instruction & Research Detachment No.2). This unit formed part of a research and development school set up during 1937 at the Döberitz training area. It comprised four squadrons and supplementary units, and could simulate a motorized reconnaissance battalion in exploring and teaching the new role of the cavalry.

It is likely that this jacket was part of the inventory permanently held by the unit quartermaster, for issue to students as required, and return to stores when they finished their temporary posting to the establishment. The Abteilung took part in both the Polish and French campaigns, before being restructured later in 1940.

(Left) This hand-tinted contemporary portrait photograph shows a Panzer Aufklärungs trooper wearing a first-pattern jacket with sewn-down shoulder straps bearing the Gothic 'A' cypher; this and all piping is in the *goldgelb* cavalry arm-of-service colour.

(**Opposite page**) Reconstruction: armoured cavalry trooper of Kavallerie Lehr und Versuchs Abteilung 2, c.1940

(**Below**) Details of the collar and collar patches. The wool piping was clearly sewn in place during construction of the collar. Again, note the zig-zag stitching on the back of the collar, holding the interlining secure between the two layers of black cloth. The two wide, flat prongs of the early death's-head badge have been punched through the collar patch and collar together.

(**Right**) This first-pattern jacket has the usual square-shaped collar, and all piping is in golden-yellow; that on the collar and collar patches is of wool, factory-applied rather than retrospectively added. The first-pattern white national emblem is hand-sewn to the right breast.

(**Right**) Originally this jacket had sewn-down first-pattern shoulder straps; the marks of the machine stitching can be seen both inside and outside the shoulders. Later, however, probably in line with the 1940 order discontinuing them, they have been replaced with doubled 'slip-on' straps with tongues and cloth bridles. The yellow piping is in artificial silk, by contrast with the original pre-war wool piping on the collar. The delicate chain-stitched Gothic 'S' cypher stands for 'Schule' (school); one reliable reference states that most staff wore the more usual 'L' cypher for 'Lehr' (a term that could mean either 'instruction' or 'demonstration'). Straps bearing these school cyphers would have been made only in very small numbers and are extremely rare. The straps are fixed with a green-painted button with a smooth embossed '3' raised above the pebble finish, identifying 3. Kompanie.

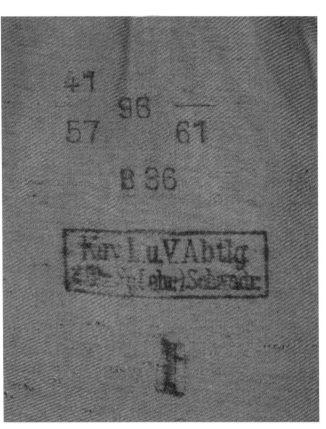

(Left & below right) The lining of the first-pattern armoured cavalry jacket is typical, and in most respects it changed little throughout the war. The factory markings naturally varied from maker to maker, but much the same layout was followed. Note the squared pocket inside the right breast, and the stitching marks along the shoulder showing that this jacket originally had sewn-down shoulder straps to prevent snagging on the many protrusions inside the driving and fighting compartments of a tank.

(Opposite page) Reconstruction: Panzerschütze, 1940. Note the characteristic detail of the second-pattern jacket – the buttons on the right breast and corresponding buttonholes on the left lapel, and the wire hook-and-eye at the junction of the collars and lapels, allowing the lapel to be fastened across and the collar to be closed.

The Wound Badge in silver on his left breast shows that he has been wounded at least three times. The sweeping victories of the Panzerwaffe in Poland in 1939 and in the Low Countries and France in 1940 were only achieved at the cost of heavy casualties.

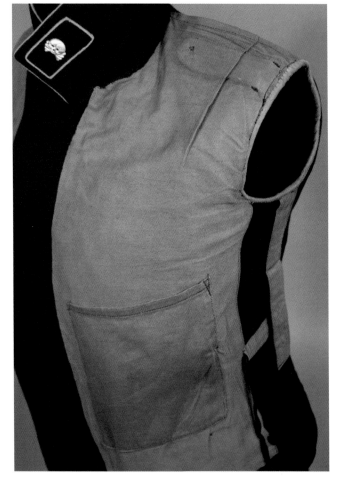

(Left) The size stampings are typical for the first-pattern jacket, with the upper right space being empty – this usually referred to the collar size, and was irrelevant on the first-pattern jacket, since the collar could not be closed. The issue depot stamp is '*B36*', for Berlin 1936; the first-pattern jacket was only in production from 1934 to 1936 before being replaced by

the second pattern. The unit stamp reads '*Kav. L.u.V. Abtlg/2 Pz. Sp.(Lehr) Schwadr.*' – see translation on page 19; such complete unit markings are extremely rare. The 'I' stamped below this indicates one of the 'Garnituren' or grades of wear, with 'I' meaning basically new. The lowest grade was 'IV', on almost worn-out clothing fit only for physical labour or drill.

Black Panzer Aufklärungs *Panzerjacke*, second pattern (Leutnant)

The German Army's pre-war programme of mechanization allowed the gradual assembly of the new Panzer divisions. The aim was to create fast, mobile, and to some degree self-sufficient all-arms formations that could operate at the forward edge of battle, with more freedom from the slow-moving logistic 'tail' upon which conventional infantry divisions were dependant. To this end the armoured divisions incorporated not only tank regiments, but also the necessary support and service units, motorized to allow them to keep up with the tanks. The division's integral infantry brigade was carried in trucks and armoured half-tracks; the artillery was towed by motor vehicles instead of the still-normal horse teams, and artillery too heavy to keep up with the assault units was replaced by the co-ordinated close support of the tactical aircraft of the Luftwaffe – notably, dive-bombers. For formations slashing deep into enemy territory, reliable reconnaissance assets were obviously essential.

As already mentioned, these armoured car and recce half-track crews initially wore the black *Panzerdienstanzug* – 'armoured service dress' – with the same rose-pink Waffenfarbe as the tank units. In July 1938 this was ordered to be replaced with golden-yellow; but late in 1941 another order prescribed a change to copper-brown for some units (this order was universally unpopular, and was simply ignored by many). The worsening logistic situation from early 1943 did not deter the rear echelons from issuing a succession of pointless orders about uniform details, which were often impossible to obey due to failures to supply new items to front line formations. Thus in March 1943 armoured reconnaissance units were once more ordered back into rose-pink Waffenfarbe, only for gold-yellow to be finally restored in November 1944. In practice, the gold-yellow piping of the old cavalry remained the most popular and could be found in many reconnaissance units throughout the war.

(**Right**) Pre-war and early-war examples of the *Panzerjacke* piped in gold-yellow are extremely rare: the author has seen just two first-pattern jackets and a handful of second-pattern, of which this piece is one – a fine issue jacket for a Leutnant of Aufklärungstruppe. The early black wool cloth is of high quality, and the lining is of silver-grey brushed cotton. The interior layout is standard, apart from a neatly executed period repair to the upper left breast which unfortunately robs us of any stamped markings. There is a corresponding repair on the outside of the jacket; what caused this damage is unknown.

(**Right**) The golden-yellow wool piping to the collar and collar patches is factory-applied. The early aluminium *Totenkopf* badges have triangular nose sockets, and display an attractive personal touch which is rarely seen – small pieces of scarlet felt have been placed behind them to show through the eye and nose sockets. (This perhaps reflects cavalry élan – similar examples are seen on the large death's-head busby badges of the old Prussian Life Hussars of the former kingdom and empire.)

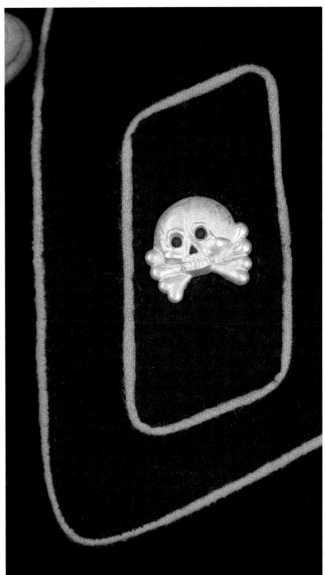

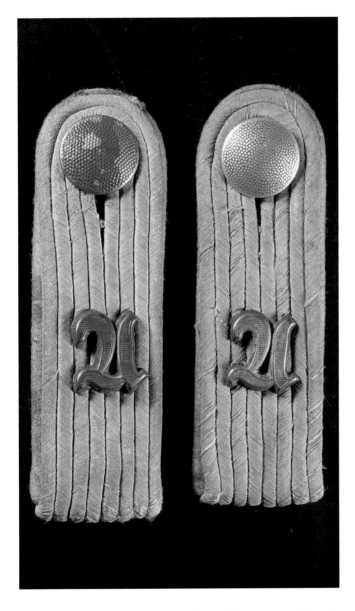

(**Below**) On the right breast is an officer's high quality national emblem hand-embroidered in bullion (aluminium wire thread), on black wool specifically for the Panzer uniform instead of the dark green base of general service insignia.

(**Above**) The shoulder straps are of wartime manufacture, topped with matt silver-grey cord rather than bright silver, on an underlay of golden-yellow wool. They are of the removable pattern, retained by a narrower 'tongue' of thin cloth passing through a small bridle on the shoulder; on this jacket the bridles have been shortened to accommodate the narrow tongue of the officer's straps. The officer's pattern Gothic cyphers 'A' for Aufklärungs are stamped from sheet brass metal with a gilt finish. In this elaborate Germanic font the 'A' might almost be mistaken for a 'U' (or even, at a glance, for the number '21').

(Right & below) The jacket lining is cut in the usual fashion, from an early silver-grey brushed cotton which is soft to the touch but hard-wearing. The belt hook suspenders are still in place, although some officers chose to remove these since they did not carry heavy equipment on the belt. Note the deftly sewn patch to repair the upper left chest area, which has been damaged. Such repairs were often carried out in the field; their quality depended upon the skill of the unit's *Schneider* or tailor.

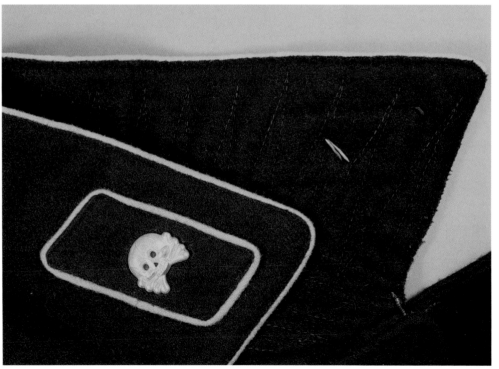

(Left) Looking at the underside of the collar, it is interesting to note the raw-cut, unhemmed edge behind the yellow piping. It is clear that this piping was applied when the tunic was first made up. Note the two round-section brass pins that retain the *Totenkopf.* These early death's-heads often have the pins located diagonally on the back, and set into small retaining wells rather than being simply soldered on.

Black Sturmartillerie *Panzerjacke*, third pattern (Hauptfeldwebel)

The Sturmartillerie – 'assault artillery' – grew out of the recognition that with the fast pace of motorized and mechanized troops, primarily in the new Panzer divisions but also in other formations, an equally mobile force of armoured, tracked assault guns would be needed to give support to the infantry in the attack, neutralizing enemy gun positions and other 'hard targets'. The requirement was formalized by General von Manstein in 1935; and the Sturmgeschütz III, mounting a short 7.5cm howitzer with limited traverse in an armoured superstructure built on the existing hull of the PzKw III tank, was ready in small numbers for the 1940 campaign. Later types would be based on the PzKw IV chassis, and longer 7.5cm or 10.5cm howitzers would replace the short 7.5cm gun.

Throughout the war the evolving series of self-propelled guns were manned by volunteers from the artillery arm and organized in Assault Gun Batteries and battalion-sized Detachments (Abteilungen), allocated to divisions or to higher commands such as army corps. As with many armoured troops who were not actually tank crews, these artillery volunteers initially wore the black Panzer vehicle service dress. Although a field-grey version was appearing by 1940 (see photograph on page 8), both black and *feldgrau* uniforms were seen in simultaneous use – sometimes even within the same unit.

The *Panzerjacke* illustrated here is a fine example, issued to a senior non-commissioned officer of Sturmartillerie with the status of Hauptfeldwebel – i.e. an Oberfeldwebel who also held the appointment of company sergeant-major or *Spiess* – an office rather than a rank. The word Spiess literally means 'spear', the sharpest point of the unit. The Spiess answered directly to the company commander, and was in some sense the 'father' of all ranks below him. The badge of this appointment was two bands of 9mm *Tresse* braid around each cuff. This particular uniform was apparently left at home for 'best wear' while on leave, and was purchased from relatives who had never met the original owner. It had literally never been worn, and was acquired together with an equally 'mint' pair of Panzer trousers.

(Right) The black woollen cloth is of the finest quality, and while very smooth is heavy in weight. The lining is cut to the standard design from an early grey-brown cotton twill, and is stamped with the date 1941. The collar patches are of Panzer style, but are edged in rayon piping in the red Waffenfarbe of the artillery. There are faint marks where a pair of *Totenkopf* badges were removed, in accordance with regulations issued in January 1943 forbidding wear of that badge by non-tank personnel. An officer's-quality Panzer national emblem is sewn to the right breast – a privilege of the senior NCO rank. The shoulder straps were missing from the jacket when found, but examination shows that bridles had been removed and the ends of the straps sewn to the top of the shoulder for a flat appearance; those shown in the photographs are contemporary replacements.

Just above the cuff vent of each sleeve is a double ring of 9mm braid; these are handsewn, and would have been removed once the NCO relinquished the appointment of company sergeant-major. There are two sets of thread loops on the left breast for pin-on awards; and on the upper left sleeve is a very fine Kuban campaign shield on Panzer black wool backing.

(Left) The third-pattern Panzer jacket had no piping around the collar itself. The artillery-red rayon piping is now the only distinction on the collar patches, but faint indentations and two pin holes show that the *Totenkopf* had originally been attached. Note the fine officer's-quality silver bullion breast eagle hand-embroidered on black backing.

(Below) The Kuban campaign shield was introduced in September 1943 to recognize participation in the fighting for the Kuban bridgehead in southern Russia after 1 February 1943. To be eligible, a soldier had to have served in the sector for 60 days, or to have taken part in at least one major engagement, or to have been wounded in action. The shield is a bronze stamping, secured to the tunic by a sewn-down cloth backing sandwiched between the shield and a metal backing plate. The backing on this example is in the correct black for Panzertruppe uniforms.

(Opposite page) Reconstruction: *Spiess* of a Sturmartillerie battery, c.1943. To the original jacket have been added Oberfeldwebel's shoulder straps of black wool, edged with the silver-grey *Tresse* braid of senior NCOs, bearing the two white metal 'pips' of this rank, and piped in artillery red. An Iron Cross First Class and a Tank Battle Badge have been pinned through the cable-stitch loops on the left breast. The cap is the correct enlisted ranks' *Schirmmütze* or service cap, with field-grey crown, dark green band, red artillery piping, white metal insignia, and black chinstrap and peak.

(Left) The two 9mm braid stripes, nicknamed *Kolbenringe* or 'piston rings' by the Panzertruppe, which marked appointment as company sergeant-major – Hauptfeldwebel or Spiess. This particular braid is a dull off-white; it has the usual diamond-patterned texture of NCOs' *Tresse*.

(**Below**) The size stamps inside the left breast are fairly typical, but with a quite large 104cm chest size. The issuing depot stamp is '*M41*' for Munich 1941. Unusually, there is a unit stamp above the sizes; it is now almost illegible, but the abbreviation '*Schw.*' for *schwere*, 'heavy', can just be made out.

(**Right**) The pristine lining of this jacket is made from an early cotton twill; later examples generally have artificial silk. Note that while the pocket is cut from the same fabric, it must have come from a different batch as it is of a slightly different shade (despite being cut with the weave running the same way).

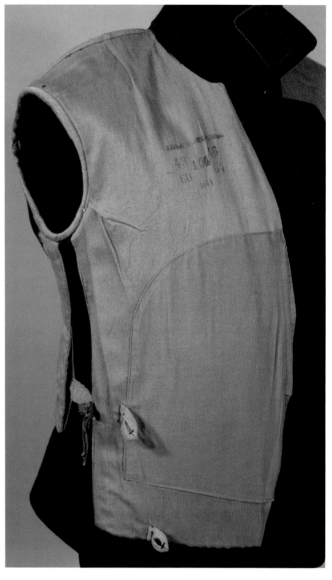

(**Left**) Here, as in many armoured crew jackets, it can be seen that the suspension tabs and waist slots for the wire belt support hooks have never been used. Vehicle crews simply stowed their personal kit inside the vehicle. Unlike infantrymen, they seldom had any need to attach the items of the standard personal field equipment – bread bag, water canteen, poncho, bayonet, small arms ammunition pouches, entrenching tool, etc. – to the belt; and with only a pistol holster attached, it did not need the extra supporting hooks.

Black Panzer Pioniere *Panzerjacke,* second pattern (enlisted ranks)

Within the Panzer division organization one essential unit was the battalion of Panzer Pioniere – 'armoured engineers'. Their tasks included demolishing obstacles impeding the tanks' progress, and helping to 'unditch' those that became bogged down; to create defensive obstacles and positions; and to assess the viability of bridges and other surfaces and, if required, build new ones. Initially equipped with actual tanks, many armoured engineer units created after the invasion of the Soviet Union in summer 1941 were increasingly provided with half-tracks instead; by late in the war most such units were simply motorized and had no armour at all – armoured vehicles were too precious to be issued to any but the true assault units.

The use of the black Panzer vehicle service uniform presented what might be termed an aesthetic problem: since the Waffenfarbe of the engineer arm of service was black, this would not show up on the *Panzerdienstanzug.* The solution was to create a more visible piping of black-and-white twist cord for use on collars, collar patches, shoulder straps and sidecaps. Because of the low numbers of troops issued these uniforms the application of the black-and-white piping was haphazard, varying from neatly tailored to almost home-made; and officers often substituted silver-and-black cord. In late 1943 an alternative piping in black with white flecks was introduced, but it was not widely used.

Uniforms with Panzer Pioniere distinctions are extremely rare, given that the numbers issued to start with were low, and that uniforms were usually worn out by rigorous physical work. As time went by and the number of armoured vehicles decreased, the pioneers were issued increasingly with the field-grey assault artillery vehicle uniform – which made better sense from the perspective of visibility, since they spent most of their working time dismounted. It also allowed a return to all-black Waffenfarbe piping.

(Right) This is a rare early example of an enlisted Panzer Pioniere jacket, of standard second-pattern Panzer design with a closable, buttonholed lapel. It is made of a fine black woollen cloth with an early brown-grey cotton twill lining; this lining is undated, but from the materials used the jacket would appear to date from c.1940–41. The insignia are positioned in exactly the same fashion as on the standard tank crew jacket, but with the black-and-white twist piping, which in this case is applied very neatly. The shoulder straps and collar patches have had the original *rosa*-coloured Waffenfarbe piping removed and the twist cord applied in its place. The collar is piped in a slightly different gauge cord from the patches. The insignia are completed by a grey-on-black BeVo machine-woven breast eagle. A length of ribbon marking the award of the Iron Cross Second Class is attached through the upper buttonhole of the left lapel; and the left breast shows thread loops for two pin-on awards.

(Left) Detail of the collar and collar patch piped in black-and-white twist cord. The collar patch follows the standard form; the two-prong *Totenkopf* has a nose socket of what collectors call the 'upside-down heart' shape. Note the very straight and professional application of the piping on this example; this standard of workmanship is far from universally found on such pieces.

(Right) The shoulder strap is an entirely standard slip-on example in black wool with a field-grey wool underside. The original rose-pink piping has been removed and the black-and-white twist cord sewn on in its place. Note also the shoulder strap button, painted grey-green over its plain pebbled finish – company numerals were one of several features which were discontinued after the outbreak of war. Such unit-specific details would have put an impossible strain on quartermaster stores having to deal with wartime levels of replacement demands.

(Left) The wartime light grey BeVo-style national emblem, machine-woven on black backing. It is machine-sewn to the jacket with zig-zag stitching; hand-stitched examples are also found. This shade, intended to be less conspicuous than the original white version, was introduced in 1939; however, the white eagle was still to be seen in use late into the war.

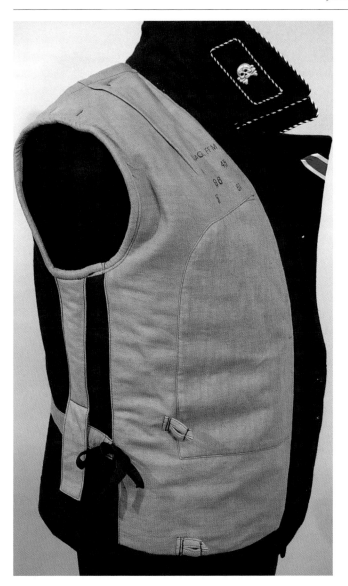

(Left & below) The lining of this jacket is made from an early brown-grey cotton twill. Note the high standard of the sewing, indicative of an early-war piece. The upper left panel is marked 'UNAG.FFM', for Uniform Altiengesellschaft of Frankfurt am Main. This corporation is known to have produced various types of uniforms from the pre-war years until 1945.

(Left) This detail view of the collar again shows a very professional standard of sewing in the application of the new twist piping. It is interesting to observe that the piping on the collar and that on the collar patch are of slightly different gauges. As before, note the prongs of the Totenkopf pushed through the collar patch and the collar itself. Some manufacturers chose to machine-sew the patch in place and to affix the death's-head later, as here; others had the machinery to sew on the completed patch in one run.

Field-grey Panzerjäger *Panzerjacke* (Feldwebel)

The need for Panzerjäger (literally, 'tank-hunters', as distinct from Panzerabwehr, 'tank security' or anti-tank units) was foreseen before the war, but almost nothing was done in practice. The German Army's anti-tank units were equipped with towed guns; the distinction lay in the need for more mobile, self-propelled equipment that could keep up with the tanks on the battlefield. The Panzerjäger I – a light PzKw I tank hull mounted with a Czech 47mm gun in a vulnerably high, open housing – was available in small numbers for the French campaign of 1940, but the need for more and better weapons became sharply apparent in North Africa and Russia in 1941.

In haste, a number of vehicles were produced using German and captured foreign guns on German, Czech and French tank chassis, and a Panzerjäger Abteilung (battalion) was added to the establishment of Panzer and other divisions or to corps assets. From 1943 purpose-built 7.5cm and 8.8cm tank-hunters were introduced, featuring fully enclosed armoured superstructures – the Jagdpanzer IV, the Hetzer, and the formidable Jagdpanther.

The crews of the early Panzerjäger I were the first artillerymen to be issued with a special uniform – the black

Panzerdienstanzug – reflecting the nature of their duties. By 1942 the tank-hunters were generally issued with the field-grey armoured vehicle uniform and would be for the rest of the war; but, as with other 'non-tank' armoured branches, there was a good deal of mixing of black and grey uniforms.

The variations of insignia within the Panzerjäger branch were also notoriously confusing. Since pre-war days there were always arguments between the higher staffs of the tank and other arms of service about the theoretical 'parentage' of armoured fighting vehicle units other than tanks; and these were reflected in frequent, pointless, and inconsistently applied changes of orders regarding collar insignia. The Panzerjäger always shared the tank troops' rose-pink Waffenfarbe; but at various times they wore the Army's early silver-grey general service collar *Litzen* on a dark green base; the same, but with rose-pink Waffenfarbe piping round the edges; full black Panzer patches with rose-pink piping and the *Totenkopf*; the same but on a field-grey base; and the same, but with the death's-heads replaced with the later, subdued grey *Litzen*. A number of variations might be worn by personnel within any one unit, depending upon when they last received uniforms.

(**Right**) This Panzerjäger Feldwebel's jacket dates from 1943. It is made from quite threadbare field-grey wool, with a lining of grey-green artificial silk. The collar carries Panzer-style patches in black with rose-pink piping and three-prong aluminium *Totenkopf* badges. The shoulder straps are the slip-on type, with field-grey tops and pink Waffenfarbe piping. A complete surround of dull-grey cotton *Tresse* and a single 'pip' identifies the rank of Feldwebel. A ribbon for the Iron Cross Second Class is sewn through the lapel buttonhole, and holes in the left breast show that one award was simply pinned directly to the jacket. For these illustrations we have made the logical choice of adding the General Assault Badge – *Allgemeines Sturmabzeichen* – which recognized participation in at least three engagements on different days, by troops who were not eligible for the Infantry Assault Badge or Tank Battle Badge.

Interestingly, on the upper right sleeve is a *Panzervernichtungsabzeichen* or 'Tank Destruction Badge'. This was awarded for the single-handed destruction of an enemy tank with a hand-held or hand-placed weapon – that is, it was not intended for artillery or armoured vehicle gunners.

Reconstruction: Feldwebel of Panzerjäger troops, 1944. He wears the jacket shown opposite, with a field-grey *Einheitsfeldmütze* M1943 and the trousers of the field-grey armoured vehicle service uniform. These units were often still equipped with open-topped armoured vehicles, and in desperate defensive battles against heavy odds – particularly on the Eastern Front – their crews not infrequently became involved in dismounted combat. This NCO displays the right sleeve award for single-handed destruction of a tank with hand-held weapons – i.e. anti-tank grenades and charges, and rocket-launchers. He wears the magazine pouches for the MP40 sub-machine gun on his belt, and holds a *Panzerfaust 60* anti-tank rocket launcher. The Panzerfaust – a shoulder-fired, 'use once and throw away' weapon – first appeared in summer 1943; the improved model illustrated here reached the front a year later. The suffix '60' referred to the effective range of 60 metres, at which its 6.6kg (15lb) shaped-charge projectile could penetrate 200mm (8in) of armour at an impact angle of 30 degrees.

(**Left**) The collar patches are identical to those worn by tank crews, with stamped aluminium *Totenkopf* and the later-style rayon piping. The shoulder straps are made from an earlier grey-green wool fabric, with a more pronounced nap than the threadbare material of the jacket, and are trimmed with wartime subdued grey cotton *Tresse* braid.

(**Right**) This breast eagle is typical of wartime issue, machine-woven in grey on green; earlier eagles were a much lighter grey or even white on a dark green base. Note the zig-zag machine stitching used to fix the national emblem; earlier examples were generally hand-stitched. Apart from those on the shoulder straps, all the buttons on the jacket are of this type, in black or dark grey vulcanized rubber.

(**Left**) The tank destruction badge is securely hand-sewn to the upper right sleeve and is deeply seated. Critical points to note when judging the authenticity of this award – as highly prized by collectors as it was respected by wartime soldiers, and therefore inevitably counterfeited – are the sloping weave of the black stripes edging the aluminium brocade ribbon, and the space above and below the stylized PzKw IV tank. This award was repeated up to four times for the destruction of individual tanks, and for the fifth a gold-coloured ribbon was substituted. It is believed that the greatest number awarded to an individual was for 21 tanks destroyed – one silver and four gold badges – to Oberstleutnant Günter Viezenz of Grenadier Regiment 7.

(Left) The underside of the collar reveals backing in a much greener shade of woollen cloth, and a manufacturing variation from the norm – the lines of fixing stitches for the interlining are horizontal rather than zigzag. The collar patches have been sewn on with black thread, and probably replace other patches fitted at the time of manufacture – a reflection of the constantly changing regulations over the patches to be worn by Panzerjäger units. Note the three fixing prongs of the late-production death's-head.

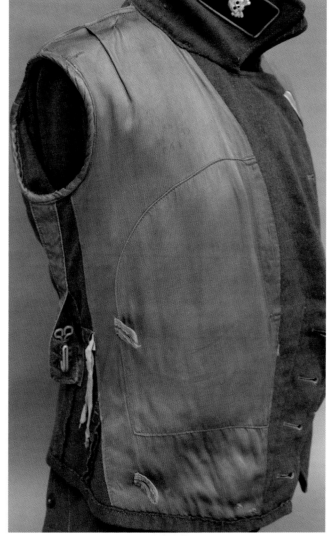

(Above) A glimpse inside the shoulder seams of any armoured crew jacket, field-grey or black, will reveal the interfacing used to stiffen the front panels and the collar. This fabric, usually of cream or 'bone' colour, was referred to as 'hair canvas', since it usually contained goat hair or the like. Its texture varied from fine – as here – to quite coarse.

(Right) The lining of wartime grey artificial silk is typical in layout and manufacture. Below the faded sizing stamps inside the left breast is the issuing depot stamp 'F43' for Frankfurt 1943. Note one of the original wire belt support hooks still engaged through two eyelets of the suspension tab; and the off-white waist adjustment tie tapes.

Panzer uniform shirt

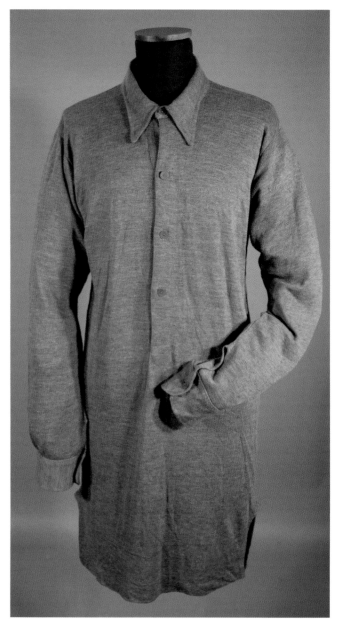

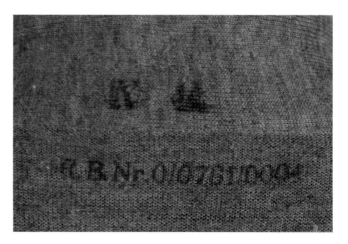

Not often seen is the shirt worn with the armoured uniform, as on page 35. Because they were readily used after the war by ex-servicemen – who kept them until they completely wore out, at a time of great shortages – surviving shirts like this one are extremely rare.

Crews were issued with this grey tricot shirt, with a long body and a fixed collar; the latter was noteworthy, at a time when detachable collars or collar-liners were the norm. The shirt was of pullover style, closed with four buttons down a long front placket. Each sleeve had a slash rear vent and a cuffband closed with a single button. In mid-1943 a darker grey pullover shirt with two pleated breast pockets was introduced; and from January 1944 this was replaced in its turn with the general service grey-green shirt of the same pattern. The tricot shirt illustrated here continued to be issued from existing stocks for a long period after the official introduction of the newer patterns, and was preferred in colder weather. Contemporary photographs also show a frequent disregard for regulations, with striped or even checked civilian shirts evidently being quite popular.

This example shows stamped markings inside the back of the neck. The use of the 'R.B.Nr.' prefix – for *Reichsbetriebsnummer* – dates it to late 1942 at the earliest, when clothing manufacturers were allocated these company code numbers.

Field-grey Sturmartillerie *Panzerjacke* (Feldwebel)

From late 1940, when ten new Panzer divisions were raised, the organization of both existing and new divisions was rebalanced to reduce the number of tank regiments in each division to one. This was a necessary step, since the ratio of infantry to tanks had proved to be too low in 1940–41. However, as the war ground on into 1943–44, the Allies began to rival Germany in the design of tanks and to outstrip her in volume production, while the battlefield losses of the Panzerwaffe increased relentlessly. Under these circumstances the importance of the Sturmartillerie arm of service increased.

Turretless assault guns were quicker and cheaper to produce than turreted tanks, and could in fact fulfil many of the tanks' roles on the battlefield, where the need was as often for supporting fire for the infantry as for tank-versus-tank combat. The number of tanks available to a full-strength Panzer division, which had been up to 320 in 1939, dropped to 230 in 1940, to fewer than 190 in 1941, to 165 in 1943, and by the end of 1944 to just a single battalion of 54 tanks. This was partly offset by increased numbers of assault guns and self-propelled tank-hunters; and the tanks of the single Panzer battalion previously allocated to some Panzergrenadier divisions were completely replaced with assault guns.

By the mid-war years the Assault Gun Battalions (Sturmgeschütz Abteilungen) were being renamed as Assault Gun Brigades, though still with just over 30 guns in three batteries. An apparently trivial further redesignation to Assault *Artillery* Brigades in 1944 in fact signified an enlarged establishment of 45 guns in three batteries, plus a Grenadier Escort Battery for defence against enemy infantry; by 1945 there were more than 60 brigades. As well as the actual guns there was a supporting park of armoured vehicles such as munitions carriers and observation vehicles. The crews of all these armoured vehicles wore the field-grey version of the *Panzerdienstanzug*. (This had originally been produced with a dark green collar – echoing that of the general service *Feldbluse* or service tunic – but this seems to have been dropped almost immediately, and the whole jacket was thereafter made in *feldgrau* woollen cloth.)

(Right) This handsome example of a Sturmartillerie jacket dates from some time after early 1943. Prior to that time the collar patches were of Panzer style, in dark green with red piping and white metal *Totenkopf* badges. These gave way to the pattern illustrated, the death's-heads being replaced with *Litzen*; in this particular case the lace bars are of noticeably large size. The jacket itself is probably of early manufacture, since the fabric is a superior green-grey wool rather than the greyer, shoddier, reconstituted material used later for economy reasons. The size and depot markings have been washed away, but some construction details make this quite an interesting piece. The right breast carries the usual BeVo national emblem in field-grey on green, sewn on with heavy zig-zag machine stitching. The shoulder straps, piped in artillery red wool, are of early manufacture, being relatively short and wide and topped with dark green badge cloth; they display the 9mm *Tresse* braid and single 'pip' of Feldwebel.

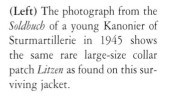

(Left) The photograph from the *Soldbuch* of a young Kanonier of Sturmartillerie in 1945 shows the same rare large-size collar patch *Litzen* as found on this surviving jacket.

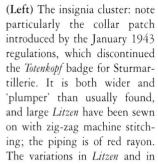

(Left) The insignia cluster: note particularly the collar patch introduced by the January 1943 regulations, which discontinued the *Totenkopf* badge for Sturmartillerie. It is both wider and 'plumper' than usually found, and large *Litzen* have been sewn on with zig-zag machine stitching; the piping is of red rayon. The variations in *Litzen* and in sewing methods seen on such patches point to localized manufacture. Note also the zig-zag machine stitching of the breast eagle; and the short, wide shape of the high quality early shoulder straps, taken from a general service uniform made before the introduction of the field-grey *Panzerdienstanzug*.

(Right) The underside of the collar shows an unusual green herringbone fabric, but with the conventional zig-zag stitching to secure the interlining. Behind the lapel a rarely seen method of tacking has been used to hold this internal stiffening flat – the sign of a conscientious tailor. Note also the narrow tongue of field-grey cloth which has been added to what was originally a sewn-down shoulder strap, converting it to the slip-on type.

(Left) The lining is of typical layout and made from a silver-grey artificial silk; no visible markings survive.

Field-grey Panzergrenadiere *Panzerjacke*, 'Großdeutschland' Division (enlisted ranks)

The Panzergrenadier Division 'Großdeutschland' was the Army's premier formation. From its beginnings in 1934 in the elite Wachtruppe Berlin, it was expanded into a four-battalion infantry regiment in 1939, and motorized in time for the 1940 Western campaign. Steadily reinforced into a *de facto* brigade with additional reconnaissance, artillery, anti-aircraft and engineer units, it took part in the invasion of Yugoslavia in April 1941. This prestigious formation was unlike other Army divisions in recruiting all over Germany rather than in a particular area; it enjoyed high priority for the issue of the latest equipment, and originally accepted only volunteers of the highest quality for the honour of wearing the 'Großdeutschland' cuff title.

After fighting in Russia in 1941–42 it was expanded into a motorized division, complete with two three-battalion infantry regiments (designated Grenadiers and Fusiliers); an artillery regiment; a tank battalion, tank-hunter battalion and armoured reconnaissance battalion, plus strong supporting units. In 1943 it was redesignated as a Panzergrenadier division, but with much stronger assets than other such formations, including a large Panzer regiment with – at first – an additional battalion of PzKw VI Tiger heavy tanks. The 'GD' Division fought on the Eastern Front in all the major battles of 1943–44, and at the end of 1944 it gave birth to a complete Panzerkorps of several associated divisions.

(Left) When the 'GD' became a Panzergrenadier division in June 1943, its Grenadier and Fusilier regiments retained their white infantry Waffenfarbe rather than change to Panzergrenadier grass-green (*wiesengrün*). The first battalion of each of these regiments was equipped with SdKfz 251 armoured half-tracks, and this field-grey *Panzerjacke* presumably belonged to a soldier of one of these battalions. The body is of a mid-war *feldgrau* wool and is largely threadbare. Economy metal washer buttons are used, but the front closure is secured with four large metal buttons painted in ordnance tan – obviously replacements from some other garment. The most interesting feature is the rare collar patch design.

(Below) On the right cuff is the divisional cuff band, bearing the title 'Großdeutschland' machine-embroidered in white Latin script on black badge cloth; the edges of the band are trimmed with white 'Russia braid'. This is the most commonly seen pattern of the cuff band.

(Left) The lining is typical for a field-grey armoured tunic, and made from a hard-wearing grey-brown cotton twill. The size markings include the central chest measurement in enlarged numerals (interestingly, this style is also found in Panzer jackets made by the firm of Holz & Binkowski). Above these are stamps of a Reichsbetriebsnummer, and the 'B43' depot stamp showing issue in Berlin in 1943.

(Below) The collar insignia are in the style of those worn on the field-grey vehicle uniform by other 'non-tank' troops later in the war, but with the rarely seen white rayon Waffenfarbe piping of the infantry. The *Litzen* are in subdued grey with green 'lights'. The slip-on shoulder straps were not found on this jacket but are contemporary replacements. They are of mid- to late-war type with a field-grey base and white rayon piping; earlier 'Großdeutschland' straps had a dark green base. Note the pattern of the machine-embroidered white cotton 'GD' cypher, and the fact that it does not show on the underside of the strap.

(Left) This contemporary photograph shows the highly decorated Oberfeldwebel Karl Schwappacher of the Grenadier Regiment 'Großdeutschland' wearing an almost identical jacket, although in his case the white-piped collar patches have a field-grey rather than a dark green base. His impressive array of awards includes the cloth version of the German Cross in Gold on his right breast and the Honour Roll Clasp on his left lapel, above Assault and Wound badges and the Iron Cross First Class. Across the base of his shoulder straps Oberfeldwebel Schwappacher wears the double bars of 9mm silver braid indicating that he is an Offizieranwärter – a recognized 'aspirant' awaiting commission to officer rank.

Field-grey Panzer *Waffenrock* (Hauptfeldwebel Fahnenträger)

(Left) Initially Panzer soldiers, like all others, received the M1935 *Waffenrock*, an elaborate parade and walking-out tunic. Of field-grey cloth, this had bright aluminium buttons; dark green 'badge cloth' facings at collar and cuffs; extensive piping in the appropriate Waffenfarbe; and bright aluminium braid *Litzen* – 'Guards lace' – on Waffenfarbe backing on the collar and cuffs. An attractive link with the uniforms of the Kaiser's day, it made an impressive display on the paradeground or when strolling off-duty, and contributed to the soldiers' self-esteem and *ésprit de corps*. Soldiers and NCOs with the means could have superior tunics privately made up at their own expense; however, this was forbidden after the outbreak of war.

Shown here is a privately purchased example worn by an Oberfeldwebel who served as his Panzer unit's *Fahnenträger* or standard-bearer. A senior NCO usually filled this position – preferably one who was tall and imposing. The tunic is the same as that worn by all enlisted personnel, but with additional distinctions. For a senior NCO it has wide (1.5cm) *Tresse* on the collar and cuffs. In addition this tunic bears an extra band of lace to make the double cuff rings marking the position of Hauptfeldwebel or *Spiess* – company sergeant-major. His additional appointment as his battalion's standard-bearer is marked by the intricate right sleeve insignia. He also sports a marksmanship lanyard, and the DRL sports badge.

(Above) The marksmanship lanyard, grade 5, with the shield for Panzer troops. Note the high quality insignia associated with private purchase uniforms, including the officer's-quality hand-embroidered bullion breast eagle.

(Above) The sleeve badge for Fahnenträger. The base was a dark green or grey-green shield shape, with the design machine-woven in BeVo style (hand-embroidered specimens must be regarded with suspicion). The badge was worn on the *Waffenrock*, the everyday *Dienstanzug*, and also the black *Panzerjacke*. For all arms of service it featured crossed flags in the appropriate Waffenfarbe – here rose-pink for tank and anti-tank troops. The right flag showed the obverse face, and the left the reverse face, with reversed swastikas. The details were picked out in silver-grey, black and white. Superimposed over the flags at the top was an Army-style national emblem with folded wings, and below this a spray of oakleaves.

The Panzer *Standarte*

In March 1936 new battalion flags and standards (*Fahnen* and *Standarten*) were bestowed on the German Army by Hitler as the Supreme Commander of the armed forces. The design, which was created by the master painter Paul Casberg, featured a field of the appropriate Waffenfarbe colour. Set centrally on this was a black Army eagle clutching a swastika in its gold talons, on a white cartouche surrounded by a silver oak wreath with gold ties, the whole motif superimposed over a large Iron Cross in black and silver. A mobile swastika in black and silver was mounted in each corner. These new Colours were magnificent works of art, hand-made with fine wools and silver-coloured bullion threads by teams of highly skilled artisans; the design was embroidered by hand on a single piece of ribbed silk mounted on a stretcher frame, with separate teams directly replicating the designs on each side.

The Panzertruppe, being part of the Schnelle Truppen ('fast troops'), received swallow-tailed standards of the old 'hussar cut', measuring 75cm X 51cm with a 25cm fork. This was mounted on a decorative wood and metal staff, surmounted by a pierced spearhead finial showing an Army eagle (also designed by Casberg). In 1939 streamers were introduced honouring those units that took part in the annexation of Austria and Czechoslovakia. Surviving flags and standards are rare, and command high prices for their exceptional workmanship.

(**Right**) The *Standarte* of Panzer Aufklärungs Abteilung 8 from 5. Panzer Division leads a parade into Potsdam on returning from France in July 1940. The vehicle is an SdKfz 247 six-wheeled armoured staff car, neatly marked on the mudguard with the battalion's tactical sign in white. The standard-bearer himself and one other soldier wear field-grey general service uniform, the two on the left black Panzer vehicle service uniform with the *Schutzmütze*.

NAMED GROUPS
Major Werner, Freiherr von Beschwitz, schwere Panzer Abteilung 505

In early 2005, American collector Bill Grist made contact with a US Army veteran of World War II over the sale of a German P38 pistol. Shortly thereafter Bill acquired not just the pistol, but also a large haul of souvenirs that the soldier had collected in Germany at the end of the war. Among these items were a black jacket and some other possessions which had been taken from a captured Panzer officer. After Grist posted these on the internet, several experienced collectors suggested a possible identity for the original owner, working from the shoulder strap cyphers, rank, and probable awards implied by attachment loops on the breast. The suggested German veteran was still alive; and when he was contacted, he identified the uniform as his.

The subject of this remarkable detective story was Major Werner, Freiherr (Baron) von Beschwitz, a holder of the Knight's Cross, and a former commanding officer of schwere Panzer Abteilung 505 (Heavy Tank Battalion 505) – a famous Tiger tank unit which had fought on the Eastern Front. The American veteran through whose hands the material had passed had been a captain in US Army Intelligence, who had questioned more than 100 German prisoners in Hamburg and Regensburg at the end of the war, and who had taken Major von Beschwitz's possessions as souvenirs at that time. The items were the distinctive black Panzer jacket with decorations, a holstered Walther P38 pistol, a mapcase, a compass and a pair of officer's boots. When contacted, Major von Beschwitz (who rose to Oberst in the Bundeswehr after the war) was 90 years old, as was the former US captain; he commented that just as the US veteran had served under General Patton, he had served under General Guderian...

This German aristocrat had served from 1936 until 1942 with Panzer Regiment 3 in 2. Panzer Division, rising during that time from Leutnant to Hauptmann (captain). In 1943 he served for a period as adjutant to the General Commanding Tank Troops/West. Shortly after this, in September 1943, Major von Beschwitz took command of schwere Panzer Abteilung 505, in succession to Hauptmann von Karlowitz. Equipped with the ponderous but highly effective 54-ton PzKw VI Tiger mounting the deadly 8.8cm gun, this battalion had been raised the previous January, and had been blooded in July at the massive tank battle of Kursk, where it came under 9. Armee on the northern flank of the salient. In late 1943 it passed to Army Group Centre, fighting around Smolensk and achieving remarkable results: in the seven months to January 1944 its Tigers – their turrets marked with their unit badge of a charging medieval knight – accounted for no fewer than 446 Soviet tanks.

In late July 1944 Major von Beschwitz was awarded the Knight's Cross in recognition of his unit's achievements in June–July while fighting alongside 5. Panzer Division. He commanded the unit until November 1944, overseeing the transition to the new 68-ton Königstiger (Tiger II or 'King Tiger'). Major von Beschwitz then took command of Tank Replacement & Training Battalion 500, to pass on his experience with the Tiger tank to new crews. He was captured in May 1945. In 1959 he joined the new German Bundeswehr, and served in various armoured commands until his final retirement in March 1973.

(Above) A large group of German military souvenirs collected by a US Army officer in 1945. At top right is the *Panzerjacke* that was eventually identified as having belonged to Major von Beschwitz; at bottom centre and right, his holstered Walther P38 pistol and his mapcase. The remarkable chain of events which led to their being identified to their wartime owner illustrates the type of sophisticated research – and extraordinary luck – which lies behind some of today's most important uniform collections.

(Right) This portrait photograph of Major von Beschwitz shows him wearing the jacket illustrated below. He displays the Knight's Cross, German Cross in Gold, Iron Cross First Class, the Tank Battle Badge with gilt wreath and plaque for 50 engagements, and the black Wound Badge for one and two wounds. The ribbon of the 'East-Medal' – the award for the first *Winterschlacht* in Russia, 1941/42 – is just visible in his lapel buttonhole.

(Below) The *Panzerjacke* demonstrates a high degree of private tailoring, as opposed to being an 'off the shelf' article. At first it appears to be simply an issue jacket with piped collar, but on closer examination it proves not to be made from ordinary wool but from a high-quality ribbed tricot fabric, quite unlike a standard garment. The waist has also been shortened significantly, leaving a three- rather than a four-button closure. The *Totenkopf* badge is missing from the left hand collar patch because the American soldier who took the jacket decided to remove it and put it on the closure flap of the accompanying pistol holster, where it remains to this day. The lining appears to be basically an issue item, however, and is stamped as such, perhaps indicating that the lining was removed from a cannibalized issue jacket.

(For the purposes of photography we have added here a standard silver Tank Battle Badge, Iron Cross First Class and black Wound Badge.)

(**Right**) The insignia group. The piped collar gives the appearance of a second-pattern tunic, despite the depot stamp inside dating the lining to 1941 – by that time piped collars had been discontinued from issue jackets. The sewn-in shoulder straps of major's rank are of parade style, with bright bullion cord instead of the usual wartime dull matt finish. Added to these are the stamped metal battalion cyphers '505' in gilt finish. Note the distinctive ribbed appearance of the tricot cloth, visible here on the upper sleeve.

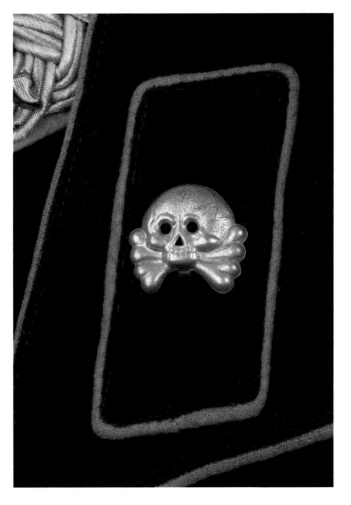

(**Left**) The collar patches are made to the standard pattern from black wool, which contrasts with the ribbed tricot of the jacket. Note that the rose-pink piping of the patches is identical to that used on the collar, indicating the same source. The *Totenkopf* is of stamped aluminium with three prongs and a triangular nose socket.

(**Right**) The jacket retains an original and distinctive breast eagle. Close inspection shows that it is actually an officer's general service example hand-embroidered in bullion on a dark green base, rather than Panzer black; most of the green has been trimmed away before the eagle was sewn down. The damage allows us to see that the aluminium wire thread is worked over a cardboard pattern, with padding under the wings to raise the design.

The generally 'as issue' lining seems to have been added to this privately tailored jacket. Note **(right)** the depot marking '*St.41*', for Stettin 1941, as found on issue jackets but not on private purchase items. The reinforcing at the shoulder seams has been made from a grey material in contrast to the standard grey-brown twill lining **(below)**. There are also two shoulder pads, fitted to run underneath the lining and interlining fabric; and some seam edges are sealed with a period overlock stitch. All these features further support the idea that this is a privately tailored jacket fitted with a 'transplanted' issue lining.

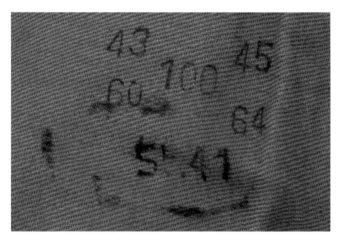

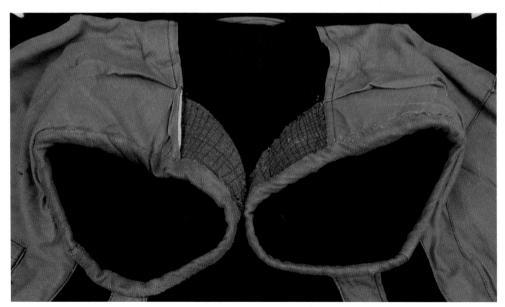

Reconstruction: Oberleutnant Horst Stürze, armoured artillery, 'Großdeutschland' Division, c.1944

Oberleutnant Horst Stürze, armoured artillery, 'Großdeutschland' Division

As already described, the strategic value of the armoured divisions depended upon their being balanced, all-arms formations that would be more or less self-sufficient. The introduction and rapid expansion of assault artillery (Sturmartillerie) answered the requirement for direct fire support weapons able to keep up with the infantry in the attack, neutralizing enemy strongpoints and heavy weapons. The mechanization of the divisional Panzerjäger units increasingly gave the anti-tank assets the necessary cross-country mobility. The bulk of a Panzer division's field artillery, however, upon which it depended for longer range indirect fire support, was still provided by guns towed by wheeled vehicles, and therefore confined to road travel – which could be problematic on the Russian Front, where most roads were unsurfaced and became more or less impassable in the autumn rains and the spring thaw.

From 1942 this problem was met partly by providing half-track prime movers for some guns, but in greater measure by a gradual re-equipment of the armoured divisions' integral artillery regiments with self-propelled guns capable of cross-country movement. A variety of weapons were protected by armoured, open-topped mountings built on tank hulls, such as the 10.5cm Wespe and 15cm Hummel self-propelled howitzers. The divisional artillery unit was then redesignated a Panzerartillerie regiment, although in practice only one battalion usually received these tracked SP guns.

Artillerymen, not tank soldiers, manned both Sturmartillerie and Panzerartillerie branches. The distinction was important at the time, and led to changes in organization and insignia. Crews of both Sturmgeschütze and Panzerartillerie pieces generally received the field-grey armoured vehicle uniform in place of the general service uniform. However, due to supply considerations, transfers, and even redesignation and re-equipment of whole units, the black Panzer uniform is also not uncommonly seen in photographs of these units.

The attempt to distinguish clearly between the tank arm and the various armoured SP artillery and anti-tank branches had an interesting – if confusing – effect on the insignia of the armoured artillery. From January 1943 all armoured artillery soldiers (as distinct from Panzerjäger) were forbidden to wear the *Totenkopf* on their collar patches, and were instead to display the *Litzen* of the rest of the German Army. The death's-head was supposed to be removed if already applied; but while many units complied, photographic evidence also shows that many did not.

These minutiae of uniform regulation and compliance are relevant when examining the surviving uniform, decorations and minimal documents of Oberleutnant Horst Stürze. We know that this artillery officer was born at Bitterfeld on 14 March 1923, and ended the war serving with the Army's elite 'Großdeutschland' Division. We know that he was awarded the Iron Cross Second and First Classes, the Tank Battle Badge, and the Wound Badge in silver for either three or four wounds. His red piping shows that he was an armoured artilleryman; but it is not known at this time whether he served with the armoured first battalion of the 'Großdeutschland' Division's Panzerartillerie Regiment, or with its Sturmgeschütz Abteilung.

At the end of the war Oberleutnant Stürze was captured by the British 2nd Army in Schleswig-Holstein, northern Germany. After the 'Großdeutschland' was almost wiped out in defensive battles in East Prussia in January–March 1945, some 4,000 survivors were shipped out of the Balga Peninsula in early April, and withdrew into Schleswig-Holstein, where they passed into British captivity. This suggests that Stürze was among that remnant; but since all semblance of unit coherence had broken down by then, it does not help us to identify his battalion.

For what it is worth, there are a number of good surviving photographs of officers and personnel of both the armoured battalion of the 'Großdeutschland' artillery regiment, and of the assault gun battalion, in the first half of 1943. All can be seen to wear, by that date, the field-grey armoured vehicle uniform; the Sturmgeschütz officers – e.g. the commanding officer Hauptmann Peter Franz, and Hauptmann Mangold, among others – display plain *Litzen* general service collar patches without Panzer-style backing or piping; while a photograph of a Wespe artillery crew shows no visible collar insignia.

There are two facts about Oberleutnant Stürze's uniform that, taken together, might suggest the greater likelihood of his serving with the Sturmartillerie. Firstly, though piped in artillery red, his jacket is the black *Panzerjacke*; and secondly, he was a holder of the Tank Battle Badge, rather than the General Assault Badge. This shows that he was transferred from a tank unit to an artillery unit; and his experience in tanks would be much more relevant and valuable for service with direct-fire assault guns than with indirect-fire self-propelled howitzers.

(**Opposite page**) This photograph of Horst Stürze is dated April 1945 on the back. Note that he has removed the national emblems from both his cap and his *Panzerjacke*, confirming that the photograph was taken after his capture by the British. He displays his award of the Iron Cross First Class, and the 'Großdeutschland' divisional cuff title on his right sleeve; the 'GD' cyphers are clearly visible on his shoulder straps. He also retains the *Totenkopf* badges on his collar patches. Close examination of the original print shows that the patches are actually simulated, by outlines of red 'Russia braid' sewn directly to the collar – a late war practice. This shows that the jacket in the photograph is not the surviving piece illustrated in these pages. It is also interesting to note that he wears the popular officer's *Feldmütze alter Art* or 'old style field cap' with the addition of chin cords from a *Schirmmütze* service cap, presumably to prolong its wear past the officially tolerated 'wear-out' date in 1942.

(**Left**) The *Panzerjacke* of Oberleutnant Stürze is a rare and interesting example, made by the Berlin subsidiary of the famous firm of Peek & Cloppenburg (which still exists in Germany today, as a department store). The material is a fine grade woollen cloth that has now lost much of its nap through wear. The lining is stamped with the date 1940. Bakelite buttons are used throughout, and it is interesting to see that after losing weight in the field Stürze has moved the closure buttons further back toward the hip of the jacket to alter the fit. This jacket by itself could have been issued to any rank; what makes it distinctive are the insignia and awards.

The highly prized cuff title of the German Army's premier division is worked in the old-fashioned Sütterlin script (which was actually taught in German schools from 1915 until officially discontinued in 1941). The Iron Cross First Class, Tank Battle Badge, and Wound Badge in silver together confirm that the original owner was a courageous veteran of tank combat who was wounded at least three times.

(Below) The national emblem on the right breast is a fine Panzer example embroidered in silver-coloured bullion thread on a black wool base. This type is in fact very rarely found: many officers simply elected either to leave the factory-applied enlisted ranks' eagle in place, or to replace it with the more readily available officer's general service version worked on a bottle-green badge cloth base.

(Above) The collar patches of black wool are of the classic Panzer design but are edged with rayon piping in red artillery Waffenfarbe (examples of these also exist piped in red wool). The death's-heads are made of stamped steel and have three fixing prongs, two at the top and one at the bottom. An order of January 1943 forbade the wear of the *Totenkopf* by armoured troops of other than tank and self-propelled anti-tank gun units, but photographic evidence shows that this was widely ignored; we might speculate that as a decorated Panzer veteran Horst Stürze may have been unwilling to remove the tank crewman's proud distinction?

The shoulder straps are the standard slip-on type for Oberleutnant rank, with one gilt-coloured 'pip', and subdued matt-silver cord on a red wool

artillery underlay. They display the distinctive and finely detailed 'GD' cyphers for the 'Großdeutschland' Division, in the officer's stamped metal pattern with gilt-coloured finish - which has largely worn off these examples, as is common.

(Below) The distinctive cuff band (*Ärmelband*) for the 'Groß-deutschland' Division is of a version introduced in October 1940, which superseded a previous pattern machine-woven in BeVo style in silver Gothic lettering on a mid-green band. This officer's-quality example is hand-embroidered in the old German Sütterlin script on a black velvet base, with silver 'Russia braid' edges. A version in silver-grey cotton on black existed for enlisted ranks; and another commonly seen pattern displayed the title in a plainer Latin script.

(Opposite page) The usual pattern of zig-zag stitching under the collar, and the collar attachment seam are visible here. On the underside of the shoulder strap note the two stiff, flat, diagonal-set prongs fixing the 'GD' cypher, and the double prong of the rank 'pip'.

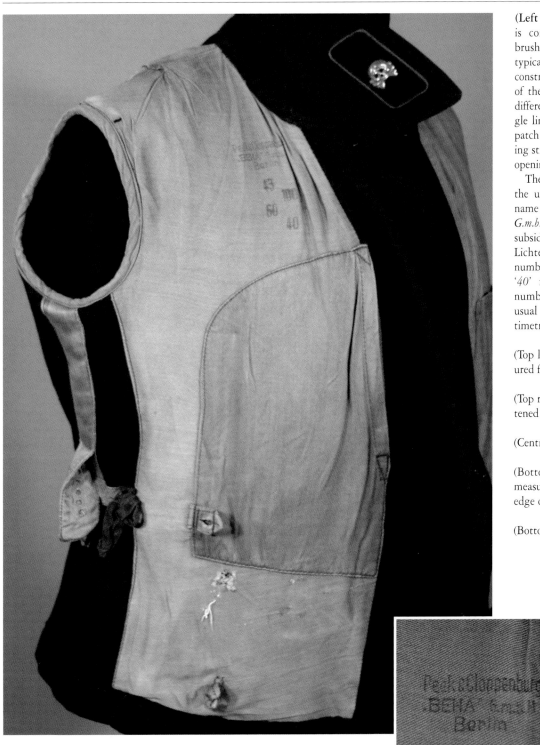

(**Left & below right**) The lining is constructed from an early brushed cotton fabric, in the typical layout. The pockets are constructed from a different bolt of the same fabric of a slightly different shade; note also the single line of stitching affixing the patch pocket, and the reinforcing stitch at the corner of its side opening.

The markings stamped inside the upper left breast show the name '*Peek & Cloppenburg/BEHA G.m.b.H/Berlin*', identifying the subsidiary firm located in Berlin Lichtenberg. Below the size numbers there is a date stamp '*40*' for 1940. The five size numbers are stamped in the usual pattern; they show (in centimetres):

(Top left) Height of back, measured from base of collar to waist.

(Top right) Collar size, when fastened up to the neck.

(Centre) Chest size.

(Bottom left) Overall length, measured from base of collar to edge of skirt.

(Bottom right) Length of sleeves.

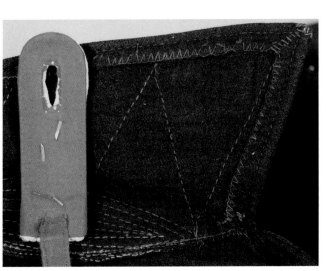

(Right) Oberleutnant Stürze's awards show that he was a front-line soldier with a fair amount of combat experience. The pin-on 1939 Iron Cross First Class could be awarded only after a previous award of the Second Class – although occasionally both classes were awarded simultaneously for the same outstanding action. This decoration has been bent to give it a slightly 'vaulted' appearance, an apparently fashionable practice observed on rare occasions. The silver Tank Battle Badge was instituted on 20 December 1939; it was awarded, on the recommendation of divisional commanders, to officers and enlisted ranks of tank crews who had participated in at least three different armoured assaults on separate days. It is especially interesting in this case, since it indicates that Stürze had transferred to the artillery from the Panzertruppe. From 1 June 1940 armoured soldiers in some non-tank branches – such as armoured car crews, and Panzergrenadiers of units equipped with armoured personnel carriers – were entitled to a bronze version of this badge; and artillery personnel whose first combat experience was in assault guns were instead awarded the General Assault Badge. The Wound Badge in silver was awarded for a third and fourth wound, replacing the previous award in black for one or two wounds; or alternatively, for a single severe wound such as the loss of an eye or a limb – which was not the case for Horst Stürze. This example shows some streaking from age.

The rear of the three awards show makers' codes; these were strictly controlled by a central organization in Berlin. The Iron Cross is impressed with the number '4', indicating its manufacture by Steinhauer & Lück of Ludenscheid. The Tank Battle Badge carries the logo 'FLL', indicating Friedrich Linden of Lüdenscheid, and the date '43'. The silver Wound Badge has a raised '65', for the famous firm of Klein & Quenzer at Oberstein.

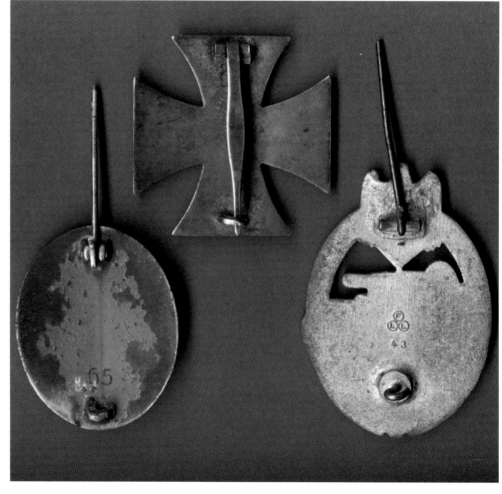

(Right) Two documents exist with the Stürze collection, both dating from his time as a prisoner-of-war, and reminding us of a little-remembered aspect of occupied Germany. After his capture Stürze was employed by the British Army as a military policeman; 8 Corps forming a whole unit of Feldgendarmerie to maintain discipline at the Meldorf demobilization centre in Schleswig-Holstein. Members wore Wehrmacht uniform with National Socialist symbols removed, and also carried some small arms.

The first document is a *Personalausweis* (personal identity paper) produced as a summary of the essentials from Stürze's *Soldbuch* by the Wehrmacht Ordnungstruppe (military police) authorities. It lists details of his general appearance: 1.8m tall, dark hair, brown eyes, and scars – presumably from his wounds – on both upper thighs and the left elbow. It gives his next of kin as his mother, Ruth Stürze, at an address in Schmalkalden, Thuringia; it records his medical vaccinations, and his wartime awards (though without dates or unit particulars). It even notes that he holds first, second and third class driver's licences. Note also **(bottom right)** the endorsement on the other side of his Hauptmann and company commander in 2./Feldgendarmerie Abteilung II, dated 28 August 1945.

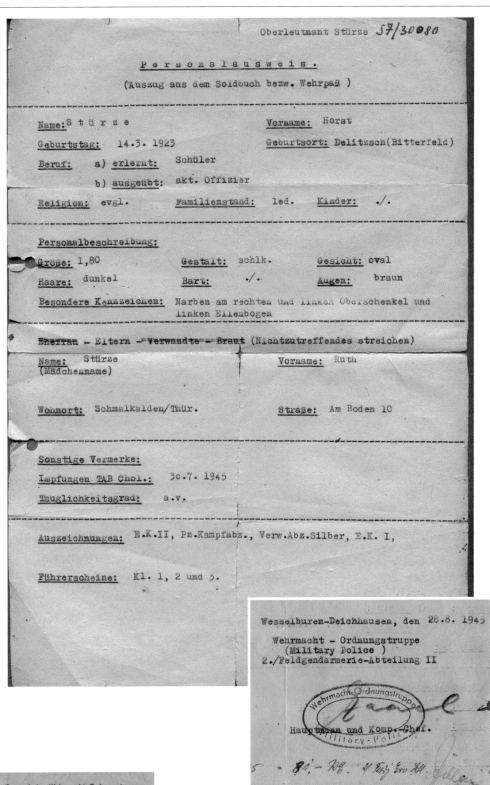

(Left) The second document is a *Dienstausweis* (duty pass) issued to Stürze in October 1945 in the British 8 Corps district, by a German military police authority designated Korpsgruppe von Stockhausen. Printed in both English and German, it states inside that the bearer is acting as a military policeman and has the powers appropriate to that duty. It confirms that he is permitted to carry a non-automatic weapon, but under no circumstances is permitted to use it against Allied personnel. His unit is now abbreviated as '4./W.O.Btl.z.b.V.' – 4.Kompanie/Wehrmacht Ordnungstruppe Bataillon zur besonderen Verwendung (z.b.V. indicates 'on special employment').

Leutnant Werner Stangenberg, Panzerkorps 'Feldherrnhalle'

The exact Panzer unit with which Leutnant Stangenberg served in the last year of the war is uncertain, since the lineage of the units which made up the two-division Panzerkorps 'Feldherrnhalle' formed in 1944 was complex. This honour title referred to an historic building in Munich that embodied a shrine to Nazis killed in Hitler's abortive *Putsch* in 1923, and which consequently was associated with the Sturmabteilung (SA) political organization born in that city. Through recruitment of SA members, the title became associated with two German Army formations, the 60th and 93rd Infantry Divisions.

The former was raised in September 1939 from Germans in the Polish enclave of Danzig, including men of the SA Standarte Eberhardt. The 60. Infanterie Division fought in France in 1940, in Yugoslavia in 1941, and on the southern Russian Front in 1941–42, finally being wiped out at Stalingrad in January 1943. A new 60. Panzergrenadier Division was formed in France in summer 1943 around the few surviving rear echelon troops and returned convalescents. The 93. Infanterie Division, raised largely from Berlin reservists, took part in the attack on the Maginot Line in 1940, and suffered very heavy casualties on the north Russian Front in 1941–42. In autumn 1942 its Infanterie Regiment 271 was given the honour title 'Feldherrnhalle', and was transferred as the nucleus for the new 60. Panzergrenadier Division in France. In spring 1943 the title was adopted by the whole division, as were the special insignia.

This new division was sent to the central Russian Front in autumn 1943, and was badly mauled east of the River Dnieper in summer 1944. By October 1944 the 'Feldherrnhalle' Division was fighting in Hungary, and in January 1945 it was largely destroyed in the fall of Budapest. (The American historian Gerald Reitlinger reported that shortly before his death in action the divisional commander, Generalmajor Schmidhuber, thwarted a plan by the SS and local Arrow Cross fascists to massacre the Jewish ghetto in Budapest, and ordered his troops to protect it; this puts the alleged hard-core Nazi character of the division into perspective.)

Meanwhile, back in Germany, the decision had been taken to form a Panzerkorps 'Feldherrnhalle' of two Panzer divisions. With both Western and Eastern fronts crumbling the situation was chaotic; men and equipment had to be scraped up wherever they could be found, and the sources are confused over the exact composition and fate of the different units of the new corps.

It is believed that the old 60. Division's Panzer Abteilung 106 was reborn as 106. Panzer Brigade 'Feldherrnhalle', led by one of the most highly decorated Panzer officers of the war, Oberst Franz Bäke, as part of Panzer Division 'Feldherrnhalle 1' commanded by Generalmajor Günther Pape. With five companies each with eleven PzKw V Panthers, the brigade's tank battalion, Panzer Abteilung 2106 'Feldherrnhalle', fought in the West, distinguishing itself at Colmar before finally surrendering to US forces in the Ruhr Pocket. Another new tank unit was formed from the remnants of Panzer Regiment 4 of 13. Panzer Division (which had also been almost annihilated in Budapest). In March 1945 the re-forming 13. Panzer was retitled Panzer Division 'Feldherrnhalle 2', and served for the last few weeks of the war in Hungary and Austria under the command of the newly promoted Generalmajor Bäke.

(**Above**) Stangenberg is shown in this photograph as a Gefreiter at some date after 21 July 1941, when he was awarded the Tank Battle Badge. He first saw action as a private (Panzerschütze) in Panzer Regiment 29 of 12. Panzer Division, on the central Russian Front during Operation 'Barbarossa'. His approval document for the *Panzerkampfabzeichen* shows that he was then serving in 8. Kompanie, III Abteilung. (Panzer Regiment 29 was one of the regiments whose two battalions were for some reason designated I and III.)

It was probably in May 1942 that he was transferred to II Abteilung, Panzer Regiment 4 in 13. Panzer Division. By July 1942 he was fighting near Rostov, before the long drive south-east to Taganrog and the Kuban – these actions are listed in his recommendation for the *Panzerkampfabzeichen 'II.Stufe'*, dated in April 1944. He was by then a Leutnant, serving in 6. Kompanie, II Abteilung.

We know from the fragmentary documentation that in July 1944 the tank commander Leutnant Werner Stangenberg – a veteran of both Panzer Regiment 29 in 12. Panzer Division, and Panzer Regiment 4 in 13. Panzer Division, who had fought all over the Soviet Union from Leningrad to the Caucasus – was posted to the Tank Troops Replacement & Training Regiment 'Feldherrnhalle' (Pz. Tr. Ers. u. Ausb. Rgt. FHH). His transfer was probably to the training ground at Mielau in East Prussia, to work on the establishment of 106. Panzer Brigade. Whether he went on to fight on the Western or Eastern Front is uncertain; however, he is known to have survived the war.

**Reconstruction: Leutnant Werner Stangenberg,
Panzerkorps 'Feldherrnhalle', 1945**

(Right) The Stangenberg *Panzerjacke* is a late-war piece of the standard third pattern, with unpiped collar; it is made from a very high quality black wool that is quite stiff to the touch. Stangenberg has related in an interview that this jacket was issued to him at the beginning of 1945. The skirt has been shortened for a better fit, reducing the usual four front buttons to three. The arms have also been shortened, with the cuff vents sewn closed at the lower end.

Distinctive unit insignia were awarded to the officers and men of the 'Feldherrnhalle' Regiment in September 1942, and to the Division in spring 1943. These consisted of the pre-war cuff band worn by the elite paramilitary SA Standarte of that name, and metal shoulder strap badges. Named examples of the Panzer jacket bearing these special unit distinctions are extremely rare. Many troops were simply not issued with them, and some with the cuff title only. Of those that were issued, many examples were lost when the division was virtually wiped out in Budapest in January 1945, and others were discarded at the time of surrender to avoid drawing unwelcome attention to the wearers of insignia with supposed political connotations.

Stangenberg's jacket has two medal ribbons sewn into the first lapel buttonhole: that of the Iron Cross Second Class, overlapping that of the *Ostmedaille* for the first Russian winter campaign in 1941/42. On his left breast are the Iron Cross First Class, the Wound Badge in black, and a rare Tank Battle Badge *II. Stufe* – second issue – with giltwashed wreath and '25' plaque for taking part in 25 armoured engagements.

(Left) The 'Feldhernhalle' cuff title was a copy of that worn by the SA Standarte 'Feldherrnhalle' since its formation from the SA Wachstandarte in 1936. The mustard-brown band in a textured weave, 27mm wide, had the Sütterlin script title and the inset edge stripes machine-woven BeVo-style in aluminium wire or silver-grey cotton.

(Below) The shoulder straps are sewn-in examples, which is unusual for this late in the war – by 1944–45 most were of the slip-on type. They show the usual wartime matt silver-grey cord, on an underlay of rose-pink wool. Pinned to each is the tradition badge for the 'Feldhernnhalle' in pressed metal. The design incorporates three horizontal 'Wolfsangel' runes superimposed over a single vertical rune, with the 'SA' (Sturmabteilung) rune at the centre. The badge is secured to the strap by two metal prongs. Officers wore gilt-coloured badges and senior NCOs silver-coloured; there was a seldom-issued embroidered strap for enlisted ranks, but this is now extremely rare. Despite appearances, the pair worn here are both of the gilt officer's type, but one has lost most of its gilt wash. The same is true of many late-manufacture insignia; there is a high zinc content in the metal, which literally soaks up the coloured wash or paint.

(Above) The collar patches have *rosa* piping in late-war artificial silk; the death's-heads were attached after the patches were sewn down.

(Below) The breast eagle has been upgraded to a rather rare machine-woven BeVo pattern in aluminium wire on black. This has been hand-sewn to the jacket after the factory-applied enlisted ranks' national emblem was removed.

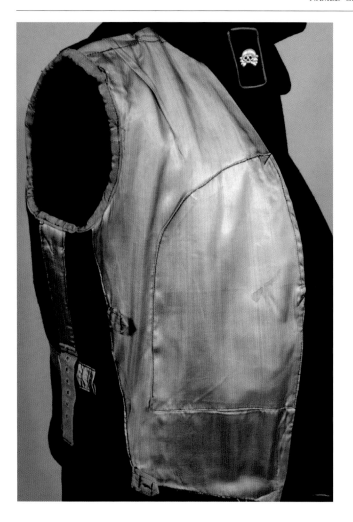

(**Left & below**) The lining is made from a grey artificial silk fabric – a typical late-war cellulose fibre. It is apparent that several different shades of this cloth have been used to make up the one lining – note the differing colour of the armhole seam reinforcements. While the general quality of materials is high there is a slight crudeness to the sewing work. The design of the lining is unremarkable, but the belt hook suspension tabs are unusual. They are not made from the same lining cloth but from an older-style web material, and may be recycled belt hook suspension tapes that were previously used on the M1936 general service tunic. The original over-the-shoulder tapes were replaced with sewn-in pieces, leaving a large stockpile of eyeletted web tapes which were ideal for this use.

The markings, rather than being found on the upper left inside panel, are actually stamped on the inner right breast pocket. There is heavy ink bleed on the synthetic fibre, but it is clear that they include the usual size measurements, a Reichsbetriebsnummer, and an illegible depot stamp ending in '*44*' for 1944.

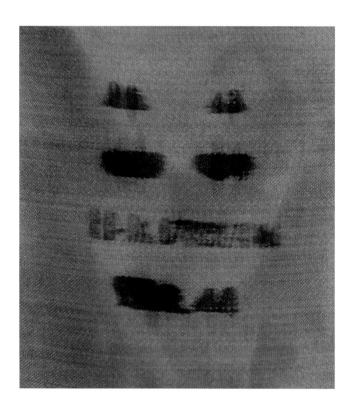

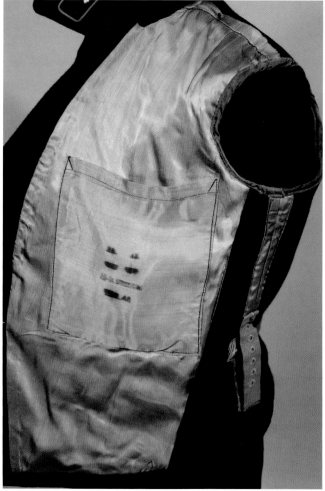

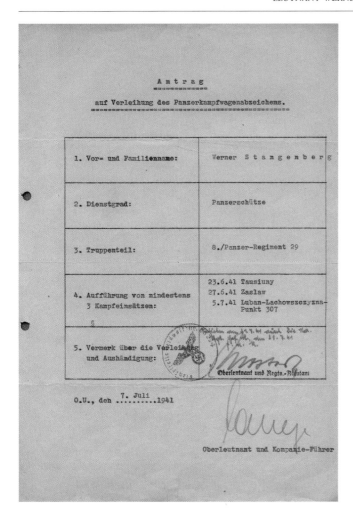

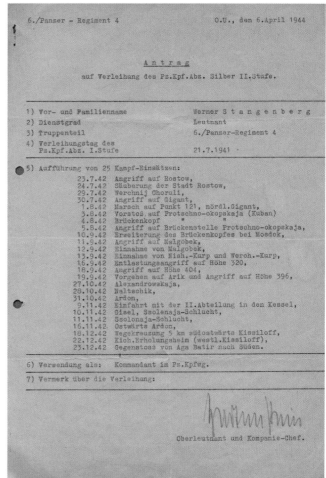

Two *Antrag* or award recommendation documents for Werner Stangenberg also survive.

(Above) The first is for his award of the *Panzerkampfabzeichen* or Tank Battle Badge in silver – wrongly rendered on the typed sheet as *Panzerkampfwagenabzeichen*. This is dated 7 July 1942 and signed by the 'Oberleutnant und Kompanie-Führer' of 8. Kompanie/Panzer

Regiment 29. It lists the three engagements which entitled Panzerschütze Werner Stangenberg to the badge: '23.6.41 Tausiuny/27.6.41 Zaslaw/5.7.41 Luban-Lachowszczyzna-Punkt 307'. (His first combat thus took place on only the second day of Operation 'Barbarossa'.) A note on the second document shows that Stangenberg was awarded his badge on 21 July, two weeks after the recommendation.

(Above) The second *Antrag* is dated 6 April 1944 and signed by the Oberleutnant company commander of 6. Kompanie/Panzer Regiment 4. It recommends the tank commander Leutnant Werner Stangenberg for the 25-engagement grade of the Tank Battle Badge – 'Pz.Kpf.Abz. Silber II. Stufe'. It lists 25 actions between 23 July 1942 (at Rostov) and 23 December 1942 (at Alma Batir in

the Caucasus). Given the battle record of 12. and 13. Panzer Divisions between July 1941 and July 1942, and between December 1942 and April 1944, it seems unlikely that Stangenberg had fought in only these 25 combats. This reminds us that soldiers holding the higher grades of Tank Battle Badge may well have been in a good many more engagements than the number on the plaque implies.

(Left) Stangenberg's Iron Cross and Wound Badge are standard and unmarked, but the Tank Battle Badge is a fascinating example. Although unmarked, it was almost certainly made by Josef Feix & Söhne, of Gablonz. The front retains much of the gilt wash to the outer wreath and shows minimal wear; but the rear shows considerable damage

and a field repair. Both sides of the badge have broken at the narrowest points, and it has been mended with solder and copper bracing strips. Such badges were clearly weak at these points, and a number of surviving pieces show cracks or fractures – see the 50-action badge to Oberfeldwebel Elsner on page 92.

Leutnant Karl-Heinz Rohde, Panzer Regiment 1

Karl-Heinz Rohde was born in November 1921 in Kassel. Like any German teenager he was a member of the compulsory Hitlerjugend; thereafter, like any worker, he joined the Deutsches Arbeits Front (DAF) – the government organization which replaced the outlawed trade unions. He commenced military service in December 1940 as a Panzerschütze in the replacement battalion Panzer Ersatz Abteilung 1, based in Erfurt. After finishing his basic training he was posted to Panzer Regiment 1, the tank regiment of 1. Panzer Division. Formed at Weimar in 1935 largely from former soldiers of 3. Kavallerie Division, the division had already fought in Poland and with Panzergruppe Guderian in Belgium and France.

Karl-Heinz Rohde was promoted to Gefreiter within the year, and then to Unteroffizier. His surviving textbooks show him to have been a meticulous and methodical student of his new profession. His division fought under 4. Panzergruppe of Army Group North during the dash through the Baltic countries towards Leningrad in June–September 1941, seeing a good deal of hard fighting as the spearhead of XLI Panzerkorps. It was then transferred to 3. Panzergruppe with Army Group Centre for the drive on Vyazma and Moscow in October. In winter 1941/42, 1. Panzer Division was ground down in the defensive battles against the massive Soviet counter-offensive, particularly around Rzhev under General Model's 9. Armee. In summer 1942 the seasoned veteran Karl-Heinz Rohde, now wearing the blood-red ribbon of the 'Order of the Frozen Meat', was sent back to Germany to attend the Panzer Truppen Schule (Tank Troops School) at Wünsdorf.

After a few months he was posted to Panzer Abteilung 116 – the tank battalion of 16. Panzergrenadier Division – as a Feldwebel tank commander; this unit's 1. Kompanie had been established with troops from Rohde's former Panzer Regiment 1. His new division had been fighting on the extreme south of the Russian Front in the Caucasus, but was rushed north to help fill a gap in the line between 1. and 4. Armee during the winter fighting for Stalingrad. On his 21st birthday, 20 November 1942, Feldwebel Rohde's PzKw III was two kilometres behind the Soviet lines when it was solidly hit by an anti-tank shell. Rohde was wounded in the throat and head, his gunner and loader were killed, and the driver and radio operator/hull gunner were also wounded. The latter was killed, by a shot to the head, as they struggled back to the German lines, and the driver died after a critical operation in the field hospital. Left as the only survivor of his crew, Rohde related in his *Feldpost* letters home that he was blinded for several days and suffered agonizing headaches; he was also deeply saddened by the loss of the men in his care.

Once recovered, Rohde spent three months in mid-1943 attending the Panzer Schule at Groß-Born as an Oberfähnrich or senior ensign. The newly commissioned Leutnant Rohde was then posted back to Panzer Ersatz Abteilung 1, just as 1. Panzer Division was transferring from a quiet respite in Greece to the northern Ukraine. The division took part in 4. Panzerarmee's counter-offensive west of Kiev in November–December 1943; and on 29 December, Leutnant Rohde suffered a second and more serious head wound, which required the removal from his left temple of a chunk of jagged steel 3.5cm long.

(Above) Leutnant Karl-Heinz Rohde photographed in 1945, displaying the unit number 116 in gilt lettering on his shoulder straps. He wears the officer's *Schirmmütze* with wire-embroidered insignia, and a third-pattern *Panzerjacke*. At the age of 23 years he was a holder of the Iron Cross First Class, the Tank Battle Badge and the gold class of the Wound Badge for a total of eight wounds.

After convalescence, Leutnant Rohde was posted on 1 June 1944 to Panzer Regiment 16 of the new 116. Panzer Division in France. This formation had been created at the end of March by merging survivors from the battered 16. Panzergrenadier Division with personnel of the 179. Reserve Panzer Division. Its tank regiment was supposed to have the usual two battalions, I Abteilung with 73 of the formidable PzKw V Panthers and II Abteilung with 78 of the old PzKw IVs; but in fact the Panther battalion never arrived – and Rohde had been posted to Generalleutnant Graf von Schwerin's new division just in time to face the Normandy invasion.

Panzer Regiment 16 was only officially formed late in May 1944; stationed east of Rouen, it was not initially sent into action against the Allies. Major Graf von Brühl's II./Pz Rgt 16 was finally committed to the doomed counter-attack against US forces at Mortain on 6–10 August – the largest tank battle of the Normandy campaign. The operation failed with heavy losses, inflicted by both US tanks and Allied aircraft, and by 12 August the regiment had just 15 tanks remaining, between Argentan and Sées. However, Rohde's unit was one of those that succeeded in escaping from the Falaise Pocket without disastrous further losses.

After refitting in Düsseldorf, Panzer Regiment 16 was committed to the attempt to recapture Aachen from US forces at the turn of October/November 1944. It then took heavy losses once again while fighting under 5. Panzerarmee in the southern sector of the Ardennes offensive in December. By now Leutnant Rohde was a company commander.

In January 1945, when 116. Panzer Division was posted to the Kleve sector of the Rhine defences, Karl-Heinz Rohde was transferred to the Armee Waffen Schule (Army Weapons School), probably as a result of further wounds; this was his last appointment before the war ended. He spent a year in Soviet captivity, being released early in 1947.

Reconstruction: Leutnant Karl-Heinz Rohde, Panzer Regiment 1, 1943–44

The estate of Karl-Heinz Rohde included two examples of the *Panzerjacke* of second and third patterns respectively, his *Schirmmütze*, Panzer trousers, padded winter reversible trousers, two belts, a mapcase with contents, awards including several duplicates, and various maps, documents, photographs and other personal effects – basically, everything tangible that was left of his military service.

(Right) Of the two Panzer jackets, one was the second-pattern piece dated 1938 which is illustrated here. The other was a third-pattern jacket marked with a Reichsbetriebsnummer, which is shown being worn by Leutnant Rohde in photographs from around the turn of 1942–43. The second pattern shown here is a standard issue piece that Rohde would have worn through his transition from NCO to officer rank, with a simple change of shoulder straps. One photograph shows him as an Unteroffizier wearing a similar but not identical jacket, so it is possible that this example was not worn in the field and has survived as a best 'walking-out' jacket. It is made from a superior pre-war woollen material, and displays the quality typical of early uniforms.

Pinned directly to the cloth of the left breast are the *Eiserne Kreuz 1. Klasse*, the *Panzerkampfabzeichen in Silber*, and the *Verwundeten Abzeichen in Silber*. On the lapel – and note, not sewn through the buttonhole – are displayed the ribbons for the *Medaille Winterschlacht im Osten 1941/42* and the *Eiserne Kreuz 2. Klasse*.

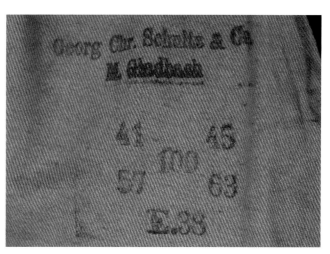

(Above) The collar and collar patches are piped in identical rose-pink wool of a fine, deep, early shade. The *Totenkopf* badges are of heavy aluminium with 'upside-down heart' nose sockets; the round attachment prongs are pushed right through the patch and collar. Collar patch death's-heads of this vintage may also be found with triangular or circular nose sockets, and with pins of both flat and round sections.

(Above right) The breast eagle is the standard factory-applied BeVo type usually found on this pattern of jacket, machine-woven in a cream-coloured cotton on black. The fact that Rohde's shoulder straps are of the bright bullion cord full dress type seems to suggest that this early garment was kept as his 'best' jacket; and this is supported by the fact that he chose to display on them gilt metal '1' cyphers – showing his commission as a Leutnant into Panzer Ersatz Abteilung 1 – of a very early Reichswehr pattern. This

had been replaced officially in 1936, but was more ornate than the newer Gothic pattern, which had a raised profile and bevelled edges.

(Centre right) The rear of the collar reveals the lines of horizontal stitching at the base, where a sewing-machine with as many as eight consecutive needles could secure the collar in one run; the number of lines can vary widely. The spacing of the lines of zig-zag stitching holding in place the interlining material also varies greatly from one manufacturer to another. Note the machine-sewing of the collar patches, and the round prongs of the *Totenkopf* pushed right through patch and collar.

(Bottom right) The lining, of the usual ribbed grey-brown cotton twill, is completely standard. Above the size stamps on the upper left lining is a factory mark, '*Georg Chr. Schultz & Co./ M.Gladbach*', and below them '*E38*' for the Erfurt depot, 1938.

(Above) This photograph dated April 1944 shows Leutnant Rohde after suffering the severe wound to his head in November 1943 – note the scarred indentation to his temple visible behind his left eyebrow. He wears the cap illustrated in colour on this page.

(Above right) Rohde poses with his proud mother, Dorothea, in late 1943. He wears an unpiped third-pattern jacket with a noticeably pointed collar, and an officer's black M1943 field cap. Apart from the silver piping around the crown seam, another length has been added to the top of the front 'scoop' of the flap – a frequently seen personal affectation. In this photograph Rohde wears the captured Red Army belt illustrated on page 69.

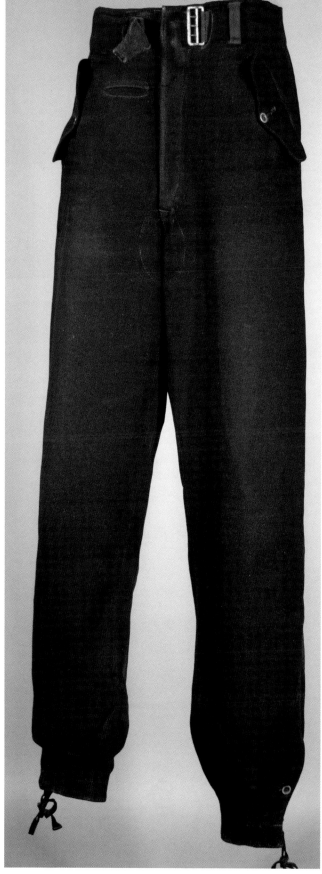

(Above & right) Rohde's Panzer trousers (*Panzerhose*) were of issue pattern, cut full in the leg to allow easy movement, and tapered at the ankle. There were three (occasionally four) pockets at the front and rear of the hips, all with scallop-pointed flaps secured with a single button. That behind the right hip was quite small, as it was intended for carrying a wound dressing – unlike the general service tunic, the tank jacket had no such pro-vision. There was also a small watch fob pocket at the right groin. The bottoms of the legs were cut to be bloused over the marching or ankle boots; they had a single buttoning vent, and two tie tapes. All trousers were size-stamped, and early pieces also bore manufacturer, depot and sometimes unit stamps; later examples like these carried the sizes and a Reichsbetriebs-nummer only.

(Opposite page, bottom) Apart from the officer's *Schirmmütze* seen in several photos, Rohde also kept this slightly 'battle-worn' enlisted ranks' cap from his days as an NCO. It has a field-grey ribbed twill crown, dark green band and rose-pink piping. When he was an NCO it would have had pressed metal badges and a leather chinstrap. Once commissioned, Rohde replaced the badges with officer's-quality embroidered bullion insignia, and removed both the interior stiffening wire and the strap, which made it resemble the popular 'old style field cap'. The interior is lined with standard brown cotton with a cheap leather sweatband; the back of the band has a maker's stamp and is dated 1938.

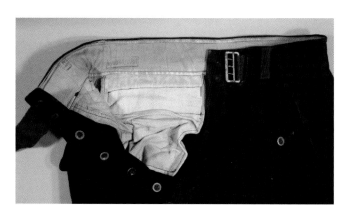

(Left) A web belt ran inside the waistband, with a three-prong buckle emerging at the left side and the belt tongue at the right. Lining and pocket material was usually off-white as here, but sometimes olive green on late-war examples. A small oval patch of this fabric was also sewn into the inside of the crutch as protection from wear.

(Left) This snapshot from Rohde's possessions shows the tank and three members of the crew that he lost on 20 November 1942 – apparently photographed at a warmer season, while waiting for help with a thrown track. The PzKw III armed with a 5cm gun seems to be the Ausf J model; the turret number, apparently in red outlined with white on the dark grey paint finish, seems to be '731'. At this time Feldwebel Rohde was serving with Panzer Abteilung 116 in 16. Panzergrenadier Division.

(Right) Leutnant Rohde's estate included two identical stamped, unmarked silver Tank Battle Badges, as well as a dress-mounted Iron Cross Second Class and an *Ostmedaille* ribbon bar. His Iron Cross First Class is made by Klein & Quenzer of Oberstein, and the back of the cross carries that company's official code number '65'. The lid of the original card box is printed *Nur vom Empfänger zu Öffnen* ('To be opened only by the recipient'); hand-written on the back of the box is '*Oberfähnrich Heinz Rohde 3./Pz.Abt.116*'.

(Left) Rohde earned all three grades of Wound Badge. The black badge is a simple stamped example, and the silver is hallmarked '30' for the Hauptmunzampt Wein (Main Mint Office, Vienna). The *Verwundetenabzeichen in Gold* is still in its box of issue, as illustrated here; the back of the box carries a sticker from the Hauptmuzampt Wein. The award is washed in gold colour, but carries no maker's mark. Also in the box (where it has left a rust mark) is a 3.5cm piece of shell fragment, showing milling marks along the spine and a stamped '1'; it is very sharp. Inside the box an enclosed note taken from Rohde's own notebook (also in the author's possession) states that he spoke on 29.12.43 to the adjutant of Pz.Ers.Abt.1, and gave his consent to an operation to remove this splinter from his head. His recovery from this wound – suffered almost exactly a year after he was seriously wounded for the first time and lost his whole crew, on his 21st birthday – was remarkable.

(Above) Documents are obviously a very important tool in the research of groups of uniform and other items; fortunately, Leutnant Rohde kept many of his papers, including several years' worth of his *Feldpost* letters home, preserved by his family. Many of the early ones are adorned with small Panzer-related drawings, or with the little silver stickers of tanks available at any Panzer barracks canteen. Through reading these letters it is possible to gain fascinating insights into life at the front.

In one letter dated 11 February 1942, Rohde writes to his mother: 'It is extremely cold and unpleasant, and the Russians are not far away. The clock I set at home in Kassel ticks in perfect time on the bunker wall, tick-tock. I sit here with very little, just my camera in my breadbag, a blanket, two coats, my weapons and what I carry on my person. The Russians got all the rest of our baggage and gear'.

Just two days later he writes: 'I am sending this to you, I hope it will arrive safely. The green fabric and the cap I got off a Tartar Cossack, and also the shoulder straps. The silk cloth I took from a Padpalkownik, that is an Oberleutnant' – actually this Cossack rank was equivalent to Oberstleutnant (lieutenant-colonel). It is noticeable, and poignant, that after his severe head wound in November 1943 Rohde's letters home apparently cease.

(Right) Leutnant Rohde's map and despatch case is a standard issue model in blackened leather. There are two internal compartments for documents, and holders at the front for pencils, rulers and mapping instruments; it is provided with both belt loops and a shoulder sling. The case still contains several maps, including the one shown of the St Lô sector of Normandy, where Rohde served with Panzer Regiment 16. This 1944-dated 1:200,000 map, covering the entire area of the Normandy beachhead, is still marked with the positions of several units, including SS-Panzer Regiment 2 'Das Reich', which led the Mortain counter-attack. Note also the mapping instruments and the case of coloured wax pencils for mapwork. The belt is a captured Soviet example, seen in several photographs of Rohde. A very clean German belt which was also among his possessions was obviously kept for dress wear while the Soviet one was used in the field.

Leutnant Günter Frank, Panzer Pionier Bataillon 19

Not very much is known about the owner of this extremely rare armoured engineer set. Leutnant Günter Frank served with Bridging Column 'B' of Panzer Pionier Bataillon 19, one of the support and service units of 19. Panzer Division.

The importance of the armoured engineers within any tank formation is often overlooked. Those without personal experience of mechanized armies tend to focus their interest upon actual battle. We forget that the daily difficulties of simply moving scores of 20-ton tanks along often primitive roads and across country, in all weathers, under war conditions, completely governed the success or failure of armoured units to achieve their objectives even before the first shots were fired. The Panzer Pioniere were responsible for a wide range of tasks, including the clearing of obstacles and mines (often under fire), and – when the unit was fighting defensively – the construction of earthwork positions; the assessment of the weight-bearing capability of bridges, and their strengthening or the construction of new ones where necessary. As the war progressed the armoured engineers were given a wider range of duties, becoming responsible for some offensive weapons including half-tracks mounting rocket-launchers and flame-throwers.

As members of Bridging Column 'B', Leutnant Frank and his Kompanie were responsible for transporting and bringing forward where necessary the ferries, pontoons and bridge sections required for river crossings. (The actual assembly of bridges from these components was the responsibility of other companies.)

In the aftermath of the 1940 Western campaign the Panzerwaffe was doubled in size, from ten to 20 divisions, by halving the number of tank regiments in each and converting infantry divisions. Frank's 19. Panzer Division was formed in November 1940 from the former 19. Infanterie Division, a Hanover formation which had fought in Poland and against the British Expeditionary Force in Belgium. Thereafter it served exclusively on the Eastern Front for the duration of the war, at first on the central sector in 1941–42, and later moving south. In January 1943 it was supporting the Italian 8th Army on the Don, and was fortunate to escape from the Stalingrad disaster. It sustained heavy losses around Belgorod in the southern pincer of the great Kursk offensive of July 1943. It fought in the defensive battles of the withdrawal from the northern Ukraine, and was rested and refitted in Holland in June 1944. After the collapse of Army Group Centre that summer, 19. Panzer took part in the fighting retreats from Warsaw through Poland and across the Vistula; reduced to a battle group, it retreated into Czechoslovakia before surrendering to the Red Army in May 1945.

(Left) A number of uniform items were purchased from members of Frank's extended family – relatives who had not known him in person. These included three service dress tunics, a tropical tunic, two service dress caps, and the pieces illustrated here: the Leutnant's *Panzerjacke;* his *Feldmütze alter Art* ('old style field cap') of the type predating the M1938 sidecap style; his awards of the Iron Cross First Class and General Assault Badge in silver, as well as his identity tag (*Erkennungsmarke*). Interestingly, the *Allgemeines Sturmabzeichen*, for personnel who supported attacks but were not eligible for the Infantry Assault Badge or Tank Battle Badge, was originally instituted in June 1940 specifically for engineers, and was at first designated the *Pionier Sturmabzeichen* before its scope was widened to include artillery, medical and other types of troops with a front-line role.

Reconstruction: Leutnant Günter Frank, Panzer Pionier Bataillon 19, c.1943

(Left) This contemporary photograph does not show Günter Frank, but an unnamed Oberleutnant and holder of the Knight's Cross. Note, however, that he wears a second-pattern *Panzerjacke* with the Panzer Pioniere black-and-white twist piping around the edge of the collar.

(Right) The arm-of-service piping makes Leutnant Frank's jacket an extremely rare piece. While an increasing number of Pioniere personnel became entitled to wear the *Panzerjacke* during the war, it was still seen in only limited numbers compared with those worn by tank troops. All Panzer Pioniere were also issued the field-grey general service uniform and – increasingly from 1942 – the field-grey assault artillery jacket began to be worn by this branch instead of the black.

The display of the ribbon of the *Ostmedaille* with that of the Iron Cross Second Class confirms that Leutnant Frank served during 19. Panzer Division's first campaign. The technical and logistic difficulties of keeping the division's Panzer Regiment 27 operational and mobile during the depths of the Russian winter of 1941/42 must have confronted Panzer Pionier Bataillon 19 with great challenges.

(Right) The Panzer *Totenkopf* badges are stamped in aluminium with triangular nose sockets. They were applied after the collar patch was sewn down by simply pressing the prongs through the collar, and these are visible at the back.

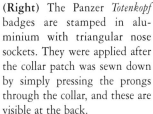

(Left) The Frank jacket is a third-pattern piece made from a very solid grade of wool that is stiff to the touch. This standard of solid, hard-wearing fabric was generally maintained throughout the war, since it was felt that Panzer vehicle uniform was to some degree a protective dress and as such should not be degraded in quality.

As already mentioned, the issue of the black vehicle uniform to Panzer Pioniere presented a problem since the Waffenfarbe colour of all engineers was black, and piping in this shade would obviously be invisible on the *Panzerjacke*. The solution was an order of 10 May 1940 introducing the black-and-white twist piping. It appears that many

soldiers required to wear this had to organize its procurement through unofficial channels; photographs show a variety of pipings, applied with varying levels of skill. Some officers also chose to interpret the regulation to allow them to wear black-and-silver twist cord rather than black-and-white; this is perfectly demonstrated by Leutnant Frank's jacket.

The *Panzerjacke* features a first-pattern machine-woven breast eagle, and slip-on shoulder straps. These latter have the standard plain black wool underlay of all engineer officers, although some officers also had this edged with black-and-white or black-and-silver twist piping.

(Left) Most interesting is the method of applying the black-and-silver twist piping to the collar patches of the Frank jacket. The original rose-pink piping was not unstitched and removed, but simply razored off, and then the new Pioniere piping was hand-sewn over the top. The remains of the pink piping can still be seen underneath when the new piping is pressed aside.

(Left) The lining is in the standard wartime grey brushed cotton twill found in many *Panzerjacke*, and is unremarkable. It has the usual adjustment tapes across the small of the back, and belt hook suspension tabs, which in this example have never been used.

(Below) Below the stamps indicating the measurements, the lining of Leutnant Frank's jacket bears the depot stamp '*E.41*' (for Erfurt, 1941). Below this is a faint purple stamping identifying the manufacturer as the firm of '*Sächs Kleiderfabrik*'.

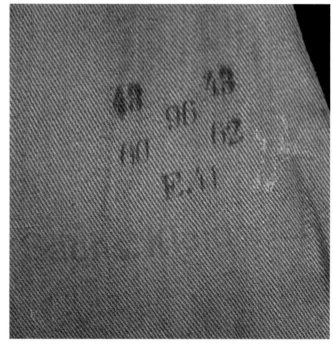

(Left) One interesting feature is that while the jacket has the standard 15mm 'doughnut' buttons at the cuffs and upper chest, the four main closure buttons are 22mm pieces which incorporate a cogwheel and swastika design, reminiscent of the badge of the Deutsches Arbeitsfront (DAF) workers' organization. The author has found this pattern of button on at least three other Panzer jackets in the past.

(**Right**) Leutnant Frank's peaked (visored) cap is an 'old style field cap', commonly referred to as a 'crusher' by collectors – to whom it is as desirable today as it appears to have been among wartime officers. These caps were not supposed to be worn after mid-1942, but they remained popular, presumably as much for their stylish 'front-line veteran' appearance as for their comfort and convenience. This example has some interesting features.

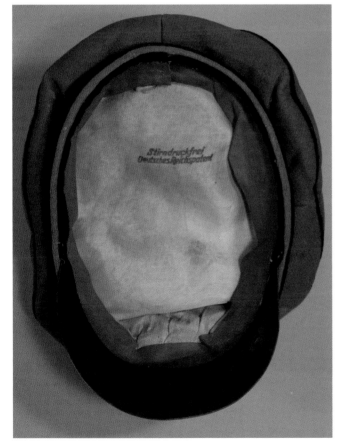

(**Left & above**) The field cap is of the typical unstiffened shape which allowed it to be folded up and stowed, with flat machine-woven BeVo insignia, and the plain black Waffenfarbe piping of the engineer branch. As usual, there is no chinstrap, which reveals a line of field-grey crown material below the band and lower run of black piping. However, the bottle-green head-band is made not of the usual wool badgecloth but of a smooth cotton material. The peak is also unusual, being made not of the normal flexible, raw-edged leather, but of a thin, soft, plastic material; it has no contrasting lining colour on the underside. These features, and especially the peak, have been observed only on this pattern of cap as produced by '*Perküro*', the trade name of the firm of Peter Küpper. The small strip of velvet behind the sweatband is also a feature of this firm's products.

Note the stamping on the crown lining, '*Stirndruckfrei Deutsches Reichpatent*', which indicates the patented method of relieving pressure on the forehead.

(**Right**) As was usual, Frank's 'identity' tag does not bear his name, but only his number in his unit's nominal roll – '50' – and to the right of this his blood group, '*A*'. The unit abbreviation is '*4/PZ.PI.ERS.BATL.19*', for 4. Kompanie/ Panzer Pionier Ersatz (i.e. Replacement) Bataillon 19.

For further information on identity tags, see pages 122–124.

Hauptfeldwebel Karl Barfigo,
Begleit Kompanie, 16. Panzer Division

This extraordinarily interesting collection of items was obtained directly from the family of former Hauptfeldwebel Karl Barfigo; they trace his military career from late 1934 until April 1945, through some of the greatest battles fought by the Panzertruppe on three fronts.

Karl Barfigo was born on 6 November 1911 at Weetzen, a village near Hanover in the 6th Military Region (Wehrkreis VI). He did his compulsory national service with the Nazional-sozialistischen Kraftfahrkorps (NSKK) – a Party-sponsored organization for promoting mechanical and driving skills. When he subsequently entered the Army he was posted in November 1934 to a Kraftfahr Abteilung – motor transport battalion – in Hamm. A year later this unit was redesignated Panzer Abwehr Abteilung 16 (Anti-Tank Battalion 16), a unit of the Westphalian 16. Infanterie Division; and Barfigo would remain with this unit or its parent command for the rest of his service.

His division – commanded by Generalmajor Gotthard Heinrici, who would later become famous as one of the last defenders of the Berlin front in 1945 – was based in the Saarland defences in 1939 and thus missed the Polish campaign. During the invasion of France and the Low Countries it fought in the decisive breakthrough at Sedan in May 1940. In late 1940 the 16. Infanterie Division was broken up, part forming a motorized 16., and part – including the anti-tank battalion – transferring to the newly forming 16. Panzer Division headquartered at Kassel (this formation received Panzer Regiment 2 from the reorganized 1. Panzer Division). The division was sent to Romania on a training mission to the Romanian Army; and the invasion of the Soviet Union in June 1941 found it advancing into the Ukraine under Army Group South.

The 16. Panzer Division saw intense fighting on a dozen battlefields including Kiev, Rostov-on-Don and Kharkov, before pulling back to defensive lines under the hammer blow of the Soviet 1941/42 winter counter-offensive. In August 1942 the now-Feldwebel Barfigo was serving in the HQ Company of Panzerjäger Abteilung 16, as his division rolled south-east across the steppes towards the Volga, and Germany's greatest military disaster of the war. The 16. Panzer Division took part in the offensive to capture Stalingrad, and was heavily engaged in the fighting for the northern sector of the city. Late in 1942, Barfigo's battalion was one of those sent to hold the easterly corridor between the Don and Donetz rivers in the face of a massive Soviet counter-blow; swept aside in heavy fighting as the Russians closed the escape route for the beleaguered 6. Armee, it was lucky to avoid the fate of the bulk of 16. Panzer Division, which was trapped and subsequently destroyed in the Stalingrad Pocket in January 1943.

The division was reformed in France in March 1943 around the few units that had escaped Stalingrad, and was sent to Italy that June. During this time Barfigo attended a senior ranks' course, and in July 1943 he attained the rank of Oberfeldwebel. He was then appointed Hauptfeldwebel (Spiess) of the divisional Begleit Kompanie ('Escort Company') – in British terms, roughly warrant officer second class; only the Stabsfeldwebel was more senior among non-commissioned ranks. As company sergeant-major of this, the most prestigious company of hand-picked soldiers in the whole division, Karl Barfigo had reached a pinnacle for any career non-commissioned officer, and

Hauptfeldwebel Barfigo photographed in September 1944, wearing the extremely rare white drill cloth summer version of the Panzer vehicle service uniform.

would have served on a daily basis close to the commanding general and his immediate staff.

The pleasant routine of a reserve formation in summertime Italy ended with the Allied landings at Salerno in September 1943. The 16. Panzer Division was thrown into fierce counter-attacks, facing not only enemies on the ground but also Allied air superiority and naval bombardment; it inflicted heavy losses, but suffered them too. With its tank strength reduced by two-thirds, it made a fighting retreat north of Naples.

In November 1943 the division was transferred back to the Eastern Front, sustaining further losses in counter-attacks west of Kiev, failed attempts to relieve the Cherkassy (Korsun) Pocket, and the retreat across the northern Ukraine. Severely weakened, 16. Panzer was refitted in Poland during summer 1944 before returning to the front line. In January 1945 it was holding a sector near Baranov on the Vistula; forced back by the Soviet advance and reduced to a battlegroup, it ended the war near Brno in Czechoslovakia. In April the division was fragmented into three groups, attempting to reach the US forces advancing from the West. Two of the groups failed and fell into Soviet captivity; but Karl Barfigo was with the group that succeeded in surrendering to the US Army.

In his later life Karl Barfigo ran a restaurant in Hamm; he died in April 1994, at the age of 82.

Reconstruction: Hauptfeldwebel Karl Barfigo, Begleit Kompanie, 16. Panzer Division, 1943–44

The photograph of Oberfeld-webel Barfigo from his *Wehrpass*. He wears the jacket illustrated below.

(**Right**) Barfigo's *Panzerjacke* is a fine example, distinguished by the 'piston rings' denoting the position of Kompanie Spiess. Like Leutnant Rohde's, this jacket too was apparently kept for 'best wear' and it in fact appears in just one photograph from the Barfigo collection, that in the *Wehrpass* (above). It is of the third pattern, without collar piping, and made from a good quality black wool with a lining in brown-grey cotton twill. In keeping with fashion the waist has been shortened, only just retaining the fourth, lowest button. All buttons are the hard plastic 'doughnut' type found on most Panzer jackets. The national emblem hand-sewn to the right breast is the second pattern, in white machine-weave on black.

(Right) The collar patches are long, narrow early war examples, with deep rose-coloured wool piping. The death's-heads are of stamped aluminium with 'upside down heart' nose sockets. They are fixed with two round-section prongs, top and bottom, pushed right through the collar after the patches were machine-sewn in place. The base edge of the patch runs parallel to the front edge of the collar – the 'official' alignment.

(Below) The shoulder straps are the early sewn-in type. It is interesting to note that salvaged wool scraps have been used for the bottom surface. Sewn around the edges inside the rose-pink wool piping is the NCOs' 9mm silver *Tresse*. Note that the straps were originally for Unteroffizier rank, and that on attaining that of Unterfeldwebel, Barfigo had an extra length of slightly different *Tresse* sewn across the butt of the straps. The two stamped white metal 'pips' also show different fixing pins, and were added one at a time as he was promoted. (The status of Hauptfeldwebel was not marked on the straps, which still bore the two metal rank 'pips' of Oberfeldwebel.) The 'P' cypher identifies the Panzerjäger branch.

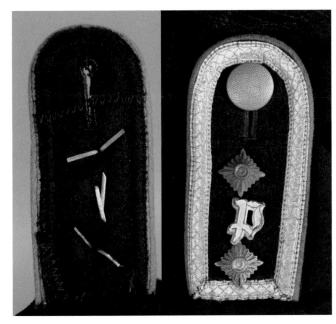

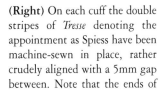

(Right) On each cuff the double stripes of *Tresse* denoting the appointment as Spiess have been machine-sewn in place, rather crudely aligned with a 5mm gap between. Note that the ends of the lace were inserted into the rear sleeve seam before being vertically stitched down. Also just visible here is the 'wedge-shaped' stitching of the cuff vents.

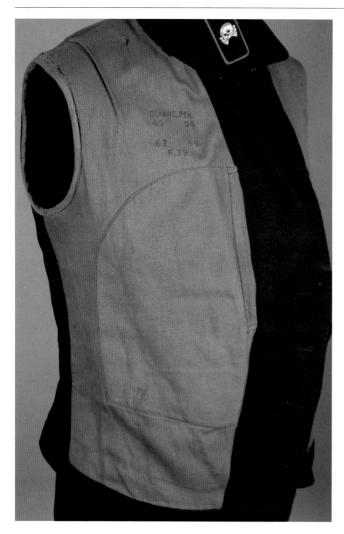

(Left) The inner left side lining shows the position of the maker, size and depot stamps. The lining is conventional, except that the belt hook suspension tabs and the waist adjustment laces and their 'tunnel' have been removed to improve the fit of what seems to be a 'best' walking-out jacket. The large internal pocket was intended for larger items such as maps, but the half-depth vertical side opening proved too small in practice.

(Below) One nice interior detail is a white stamping below and behind the left armhole showing the manufacturer of the black woollen cloth from which the jacket was made. These white stencils were applied at the ends of large bolts of cloth. This example shows a sizeable and ornate crest above the name 'Michelstadt'; this town, just south-east of Frankfurt, had several textile mills. The present author has examined another Panzer jacket from the same manufacturer which also carries the same textile stencil.

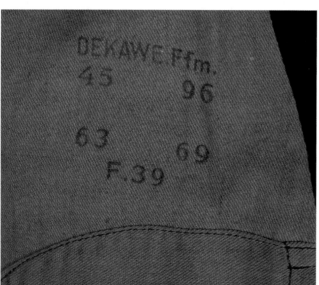

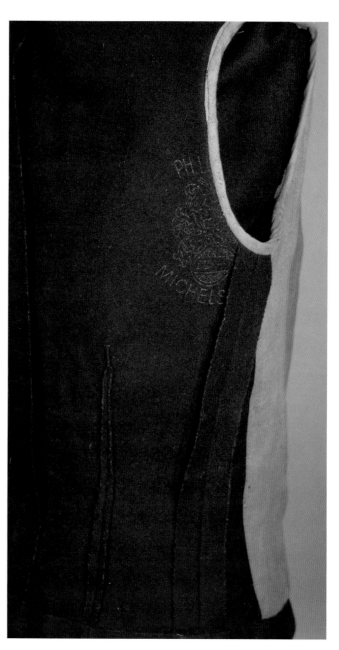

(Above) On the left breast above the size stamps the lining is marked 'DEKAWE Ffm', which actually stands for the KaDeWe department store. Like the Peek & Cloppenburg chain, this concern also manufactured uniforms for the Wehrmacht. 'Ffm' is the acronym for Frankfurt-am-Main; and the issuing depot's stamp at the bottom is 'F39' for Frankfurt, 1939. A unique detail of this particular manufacturer's markings is that the chest measurement (here '96') is not central, but at upper right.

(Left & below left) Although it now bears the insignia of his highest rank, Karl Barfigo had this *Waffenrock* privately tailored by Dietrich Bruse of Hamm – then the garrison of Panzer Abwehr Abteilung 16 – when he reached the rank of Unteroffizier in 1937. The tunic is made of officer's-quality field-grey wool tricot, with superior insignia; the breast eagle, hand-embroidered in bullion, is one of the finest examples this author has ever seen. Again, the shoulder straps have been up-graded in rank to Oberfeldwebel by the addition of an extra strip of *Tresse* across the butt and two metal 'pips'; they display the stamped white metal '*16*' cyphers of Barfigo's battalion. Three medal ribbons on a short bar are pinned to the left breast, for the War Service Cross with Swords, the *Ostmedaille*, and the Army Four Years' Service Medal. No thread loops have been added to take other decorations.

(Below) Snapshot of the 26-year-old Unteroffizier Barfigo wearing his *Waffenrock*. Just visible on the shoulder straps are the rose-pink embroidered cyphers appropriate to his rank and unit at that date – '*P*' over '*16*'.

The awards made to Karl Barfigo are listed in his *Wehrpass*. They were (in chronological order):

Four Years' Service Medal, War Service Cross Second Class with Swords, 1941/42 Eastern Winter Medal, War Service Cross First Class with Swords, Wound Badge in black, General Assault Badge, tradition cap badge of 16. Panzer Division with certificate, Iron Cross Second Class, and Close Combat Clasp in bronze. It is particularly interesting to note that the divisional tradition badge was held in such esteem that it was officially listed as an award and accompanied by a document.

(**Left & below**) The surviving selection of awards are illustrated, in place on the *Panzerjacke* and from the reverse. The first issue Close Combat Clasp in bronze is marked on the rear with the designer's name '*F.E.C.W. Peekhaus/Berlin*', and the manufacturer's logo, '*FFL*' in three circles, for Friedrich Linden of Lüdenscheid. Note the wide pin and the crimped-in backing plate. Below this is a simple medal bar showing the ribbons of the War Service Cross Second Class with Swords, the 1941/42 Eastern Winter Medal, and the Four Years' Service Medal. Centred below this is the War Service Cross First Class with Swords, marked '3' on the back for Wilhelm Deumer of Lüdenscheid; the cross is well worn and has a broken pin at the rear. Lower left is the General Assault Badge; while unmarked, this was probably made by Steinhauer & Lück of Lüdenscheid. The black Wound Badge is unmarked.

(**Above**) Hauptfeldwebel Barfigo, wearing field-grey general service uniform, is seen presenting documents to Generalmajor Dietrich von Müller, commander of 16. Panzer Division from August 1944 to April 1945. Note on the left side of Barfigo's M1943 cap the shield-shaped divisional tradition badge – sadly, not now part of this collection. It was grey with a yellow rim, enclosing the yellow divisional vehicle sign of a Y-rune with a short crossbar near the bottom.

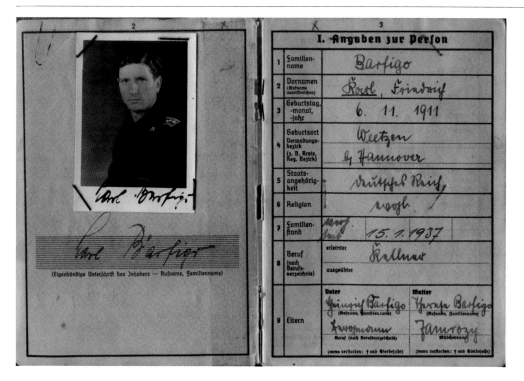

(Left) The front page of Barfigo's *Wehrpass* shows him in the black Panzer jacket; it bears his signature on the photograph and a counter-signature below. The photo had to show the individual clearly and bareheaded, but it is not unusual to find examples where they are shown in civilian dress. Opposite are the basic details: names, birth date and place, next of kin, etc. This book was re-made in late 1941 to replace an earlier one.

The *Wehrpass* was the personal identity book for all men of conscriptable age. It was presented when the recipient registered, and if he subsequently joined a Wehrmacht unit the *Wehrpass* was then deposited in the unit records and he was given a pay-book – *Soldbuch* – to carry in place of it. The *Wehrpass* was only returned when the recipient left the service, or else it was returned to his next of kin in case of his death. The booklet was progressively filled in with all relevant details of service: unit postings, pay grades, training courses undertaken, ranks attained, military actions taken part in, awards, and many other details. In short, it is a concise but complete accounting of a soldier's service; and as such, it is a fascinating and invaluable asset for collectors researching a uniform.

(Left) Page 12 shows all the units the recipient has served in. Some units had stamps made for this purpose, but most entries will be handwritten. Barfigo's service shows a direct line from 1. Kompanie/Kraftfahr Abteilung Hamm in November 1934, to Panzer Abwehr Abteilung 16 in October 1935, to Panzerjäger Abteilung 16 in April 1940, to the Begleit Kompanie, 16. Panzer Division in July 1943.

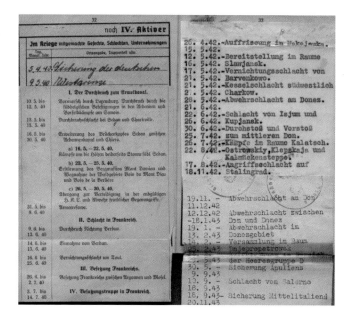

(Right) The soldier's combat service is listed on pages 32 & 33. Some earlier entries will be hand written, but as the war went on units had printed or typed sheets made up to paste in. In Barfigo's *Wehrpass* these amount to several overlapping gatefold pages, sprinkled with the names of famous battlefields such as Sedan, Kiev, Kharkov, and, half way down page 33, '17.8.42-18.11.42 – Attack on Stalingrad'. At the bottom of the page we see '10.9.-18.9.43 – Battle of Salerno'.

(Above) Hauptfeldwebel Barfigo, right, at Cupello in Italy, summer 1943, just before the Allied landings at Salerno; he wears tropical shirtsleeve order and high-lacing Italian paratrooper boots. Note the Begleit Kompanie's metal pennant at far right. In the top corner it bears the divisional sign; in the centre, the tactical sign for a motorized company, topped with a staff flying a command streamer above a pennant; the damaged lettering at left may read '*Kp. Chef*' .

(Above) Poland, summer 1944 – another photo of Barfigo wearing the exceptionally rare white drill Panzer uniform with applied full-colour insignia. This outfit was quickly replaced by one made in reed-green or mouse-grey. The portly Stabsfeldwebel at left is so determined to wear this Sturmartillerie jacket that he has 'expanded' it by moving the right hand buttons almost to the centre front.

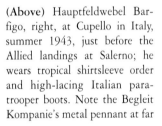

(Above) Barfigo wears the white drill uniform – note large left thigh pocket – while saying a few words over the grave of Oberfähnrich Karl-Heinz Behnsen of the Begleit Kompanie, killed on 20 August 1944 at Gnojno, Poland.

(Above) Barfigo, wearing the two cuff rings of the Spiess or Hauptfeldwebel, poses at the head of a line-up of Begleit Kompanie officers and NCOs. Most wear the general service tunic, but two have the grey assault artillery jacket. The pennant that Barfigo carries differs from that in the photo at top left; it seems to bear the words '*Stoss Führer*' – 'shock leader'?

Reconstruction: Oberfeldwebel Herbert Elsner, Panzer Regiment 23, 1944

Oberfeldwebel Herbert Elsner, Panzer Regiment 23

Herbert Elsner was sworn in for 12 years' service as a volunteer in the German Army on 16 November 1937, as a member of 2. Kompanie/Panzer Regiment 5 at Wünsdorf, Berlin – the base of 3. Panzer Division, commanded by the great tank general Leo, Freiherr Geyr von Schweppenburg. It was the start of a remarkable and distinguished career in the Panzertruppe, of which his surviving uniform decorations, photographs and documents provide a fascinating record.

Elsner would remain with Panzer Regiment 5 from 1937 until the beginning of 1941, rising from Panzerschütze to Unteroffizier (sergeant). He took part in the annexation of Czechoslovakia, and saw combat in the invasions of Poland, the Low Countries and France. During the reorganization and expansion of the Panzerwaffe in winter 1940/41 his division gave up several combat units, including Panzer Regiment 5, to 5. leichte Division (soon to transfer to North Africa and to become 21. Panzer Division). However, it was not Unteroffizier Elsner's destiny to sweat under the desert sun in the ranks of the Afrikakorps. During the extensive cross-postings in January 1941 he was transferred to the unit with which he would see out the rest of the war, fighting exclusively on the Eastern Front: Panzer Regiment 201, later redesignated Panzer Regiment 23.

Elsner's new unit was the tank regiment for 23. Panzer Division, formed in France between September 1941 and March 1942 under the command of another aristocratic cavalryman, Generalmajor Hans, Freiherr von Boineburg-Lengsfeld. Herbert Elsner missed the opening campaigns of Operation 'Barbarossa'; but in April 1942 the 23. Panzer made the long journey eastwards to the Ukraine, arriving in time to see heavy fighting around Kharkov against the Russian spring offensive. The division subsequently took part in most of the great battles on the Eastern Front, suffering heavy losses again and again. In summer 1942 it drove deep into the Caucasus, reaching the Terek river – the furthest into the USSR that the Wehrmacht ever penetrated. Rushed north again to take part in the doomed attempt by 4. Panzerarmee to relieve encircled Stalingrad, Panzer Regiment 23 had been worn down to 20 tanks by January 1943. Re-equipped and brought up to strength, it fought in the Ukraine throughout the rest of that year.

By winter 1943/44, Herbert Elsner had reached the rank of Feldwebel (sergeant) and was commander of a PzKw V Panther tank in the headquarters company of his regiment's II Abteilung. He had a lucky escape during the defensive battles round Krivoi Rog, where his division fought repeated actions between November 1943 and March 1944. His Panther took an anti-tank round in the turret and was also immobilized with a broken track, in full view of the enemy. Red Army infantry armed with 'Molotov cocktails' rushed forward; Elsner related, *'At that moment I looked out of the turret directly into the eyes of a Russian. Quickly I got my gun from the turret, and shot him down.'* The Panther then destroyed a further two Soviet 122mm guns, before backing away in search of some cover, crabbing along on its broken track.

By the next day repairs had been made, and the crew mounted to leave; but just as Oberfeldwebel Elsner was about to give the order to start up, a shell exploded on the rear engine deck, blowing away stowage bins and camouflage and throwing two of the dismounted crew clear of the tank. They were shaken

Zur Erinnerung an meine Dienstzeit

but uninjured, and the Panther finally got under way. Soon afterwards they encountered two T-34 tanks, which they destroyed at close range. In these actions Elsner, with a handful of other tanks, had defended 2 kilometres of the divisional front for several days, stopping a Soviet tank breakthrough into the rear of the division's Panzergrenadier Regiment 126. (For his command during this episode Elsner's officer, Leutnant Gerhard Fischer, received the Knight's Cross.)

Oberfeldwebel Elsner would see further combat during the furious battles in the Dnieper Bend, around Jassy in Romania, on the retreat through Poland, and then in a German counter-offensive in Hungary in October 1944. His division remained in Hungary until April 1945; and although it was almost wiped out on the shores of Lake Balaton, some remnants of 23. Panzer managed to limp across the border into Austria, where they surrendered to British forces early in May. Among the few remaining survivors of more than six years of tank warfare was Oberfeldwebel Herbert Elsner of the Stabskompanie, II. Abteilung/Panzer Regiment 23.

(Opposite page) Oberfeldwebel Elsner in a posed portrait photograph dating from mid-1944, wearing a piped-collar second-pattern *Panzerjacke*. Note the officer's-quality bullion breast eagle. The photographer's studio address is given as 41 Adolf Hitlerstrasse, Kornwestheim – so this was taken while Elsner was on leave, and no doubt wearing his best walking-out uniform.

(Right) A snapshot from among Elsner's souvenirs shows two of his comrades, one of them wearing a jacket which provides a most interesting comparison with the Elsner *Panzerjacke* illustrated below: the Spiess on the right wears a second-pattern jacket which has been re-tailored to take a zip fastener down the front centre. The sergeant-major's *Einheitsfeldmütze* dates the photo – and thus perhaps the fashion for zippers in Pz Rgt 23? – to mid-1943 at the earliest.

(Left) Oberfeldwebel Elsner's jacket is a remarkable example of a 'personalized' *Panzerjacke*. Its most immediately striking feature is that at some time late in the war he has had the lapels and the 'wrap-around' of the left front panel removed, the skirt considerably shortened, new slash pockets cut into the front, and a zip fastener added – thus turning the issue garment into a very smart, functional (and surprisingly modern-looking) single-breasted battle jacket. Such a modification is very rarely seen, and the evidence (above) that another senior NCO of Elsner's regiment had a jacket re-tailored in a similar way can hardly be a simple coincidence.

The original jacket is a standard mid-war third-pattern example; the markings on the brushed cotton lining have been completely washed away, so the exact year of issue cannot be confirmed. Note the small, slanting slash pockets added low on the ribs at each side; the pocket bags are made from scrap lining fabric in several patterns.

The attached awards are the German Cross in Gold, the Iron Cross First Class and the Tank Battle Badge for 50 engagements. The ribbon bar is for the annexation of Czechoslovakia, and below this is a diamond-shaped Hitler Youth badge.

(Right) The collar appears to be of a slightly different shade to the rest of the jacket, or seems to have been made from a different bolt of cloth which has aged differently. The collar patches are in black wool with rose-pink rayon piping. The aluminium *Totenkopf* badges have triangular nose sockets, and two stiff, flat fixing pins are pushed through the patch and collar alike. The shoulder straps are seen in earlier photographs of Elsner wearing a second-pattern jacket, and have obviously been carried through to this jacket. Note the contrast between the smooth rayon piping on the collar patches and the more heavily textured piping on the shoulder straps – this ribbed effect is not often seen on Panzer straps.

(Left) The BeVo machine-woven breast eagle is a second-pattern piece in white on black; these were later discontinued in favour of light grey. It is machine-sewn to the jacket.

The *Deutsche Kreuz in Gold* is the version with a metal central motif on a stitched cloth background star – grey, for Army personnel. This piece was among Elsner's possessions; he was awarded this decoration – which ranked between the Iron Cross First Class and the Knight's Cross – on 2 March 1944, after the battles around Krivoi Rog. Here it is lightly tacked to the jacket in place of his metal version of the order, which is now in another collection. Mounting loops for the pin of the metal decoration exist behind the cloth example shown here.

(Right) The well worn slip-on shoulder straps that Elsner wore on more than one jacket; the first digit of the white metal regimental cypher '23' is missing from one strap. The brass attachment pins for the rank 'pips' and cyphers can clearly be seen. The straps have the usual complete *Tresse* edging that marked ranks from Unterfeldwebel upwards. Note also the curious strip of silver 'Russia braid' around the butt of the straps. This may perhaps be worn to distinguish the Kompanie, since it is visible in several photos of other personnel. It is unlikely to indicate an officer candidate, since that status was identified by a double loop of *Tresse* round the end of the straps.

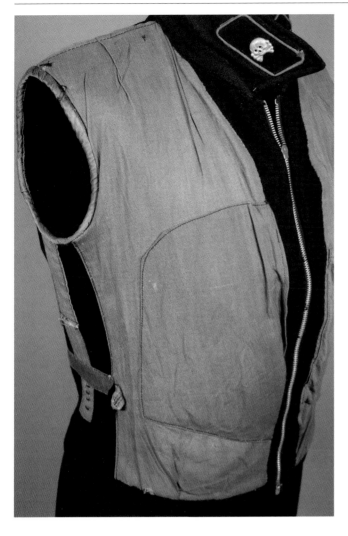

(Left) The lining of Elsner's jacket is made from a grey brushed cotton fabric typical of early- to mid-war examples. The extensive re-tailoring can be seen here, with the new single-breasted front and zipper, and the skirt drastically shortened. Note that the lower internal buttonhole tab is no longer present, and the hanging strips for the belt hooks have been removed. A snug fit and short waist were considered quite fashionable.

(Right) Detail of the 'ZIPP' brand zip fastener, with a chain-and-ball pull tag.

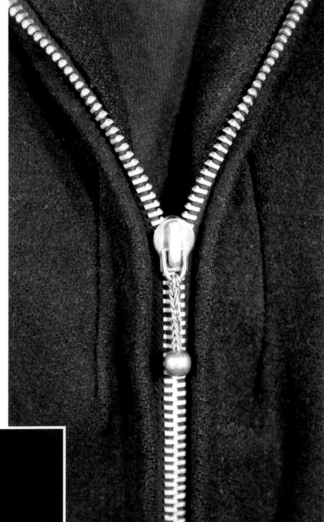

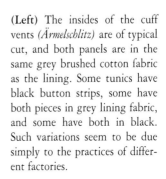

(Left) The insides of the cuff vents *(Ärmelschlitz)* are of typical cut, and both panels are in the same grey brushed cotton fabric as the lining. Some tunics have black button strips, some have both pieces in grey lining fabric, and some have both in black. Such variations seem to be due simply to the practices of different factories.

(Left) Elsner with the crew of his PzKw V Panther. This was not normally issued to the second battalion of Panzer regiments, which usually kept the later models of the PzKw IV; but the Stabskompanie, II./Pz Rgt 23 was clearly an exception.

(Bottom left) Elsner sitting in one of his unit's Schwimmwagen amphibious field cars. His black M1943 cap appears to have a metal eagle, a cockade on a diamond-shaped *feldgrau* backing, and the 23. Panzer Division tradition badge just visible on the left side (see page 99). Elsner wears the third-pattern black jacket with padded, reversible winter overtrousers (either camouflage-printed, or perhaps just a very stained pair of the early grey type?); the enlisted man beside him wears the field-grey assault artillery uniform. Elsner displays the array of awards seen on page 87, with his Iron Cross Second Class ribbon and – at this date – the standard silver Tank Battle Badge.

(Below) A close-up of Feldwebel Elsner in the turret of his Panther; note the drum-type cupola of this early Ausf D version. Although much splashed with mud, it appears to be in plain all-over factory ochre-yellow finish, and shows no Zimmerit anti-magnetic plaster. The turret marking, in red outlined with white, seems to be 'II A 1'. This clearly indicates the Stabskompanie of II Abteilung; the individual tank number may perhaps have a second digit, hidden here by the spare track plates on the turret.

(This page) Three excellent snapshots from Herbert Elsner's collection, dating from late 1943 or early 1944 when his unit was operating around Krivoi Rog in the southern Ukraine. In all of these photos Feldwebel Elsner appears to be wearing a conventional, unmodified third-pattern *Panzerjacke*.

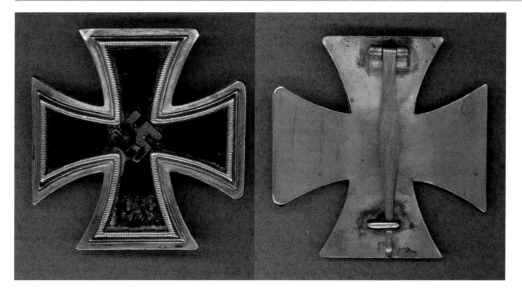

(Left) Elsner's Iron Cross First Class is a very worn example, having been on his jacket since its award on 11 October 1942. It shows what seems to be a '3' below the hook; if so, the manufacturer was Wilhelm Deumer of Lüdensheid. Elsner apparently scratched his initials on the back, 'H' with a stylized 'E'.

(Right & below) Perhaps the most remarkable feature of the whole Elsner group is convincing evidence that he was in fact an 'unofficial' winner of the Knight's Cross. From the closing days of the war there are a number of accounts of outstanding soldiers being recommended for this coveted decoration, but failing to actually receive it due to the chaotic situation in the collapsing Third Reich. Often, in modest front-line ceremonies staged by their comrades, such soldiers would receive instead an Iron Cross Second Class modified so that it could be worn at the throat like the genuine *Ritterkreuz*. Elsner related that just such a decoration was awarded

to him at the front and he later received a simple document of confirmation.

Above the stamp of Panzer Regiment 23 and the signature of its CO from 14 March 1945, Oberstleutnant Jahns, this states that 'It is hereby certified that Oberfeldwebel Herbert Elsner, Stabskp.II./Pz. Rgt. 23, was bestowed with the Knight's Cross of the Iron Cross on 10 April 1945'. It is dated 21 May 1945, when the unit had been in captivity for about two weeks but was not yet demobilized. No reference to the award was entered in Elsner's *Wehrpass*; but this convincing document cannot be dismissed lightly.

(Above) The award presented to Oberfeldwebel Elsner: an Iron Cross Second Class with a makeshift steel wire loop fitted to the bent suspension ring. The *EK II* is 44mm x 44mm – at a glance, an adequate substitute for the 48mm x 48mm *Ritterkreuz*. It is well documented that such substitutes were in any case often worn in the field, to avoid the risk of losing the precious original Knight's Cross.

(**Right**) On 2 March 1944 Elsner was presented with the German Cross in Gold. His star shows signs of having been worn continuously in the last year of the war. The rear of the pin is marked '20', the code for the manufacturer C.F.Zimmermann of Pforzheim. Although nick-named 'The Fried Egg', the *Deutsches Kreuz* was a desirable decoration, seen as a stepping-stone linking the award of the Iron Cross First Class with that of the Knight's Cross.

(**Left**) Elsner received the *Panzerkampfabzeichen* for 50 assaults on 16 April 1944 – this was the so-called 'III. Stufe' or third award. He had already received the 25-action badge (II. Stufe) on 12 December 1943. The badge is well worn, evidence of a hard life at the front, and the frame has broken on one side, where the headlight of the tank crosses the wreath – a very common mishap with this pattern of badge. The reverse is unmarked.

(**Right**) Elsner's Tank Battle Badge for 75 actions, awarded on 1 April 1945 – the very rare 'IV. Stufe' or fourth award. The very solidly made badge is a classic example of the products of 'JFS' (Josef Feix & Söhne, of Gablonz adN). The metal used in these later badges often soaks up the gold wash finish used on the wreaths, as seen here.

Reconstruction: Oberfeldwebel Richard Alber, Panzer Aufklärungs Abteilung 23, 1944

Oberfeldwebel Richard Alber, Panzer Aufklärungs Abteilung 23

Given that mobility, and a spearhead role in the assault, was the key to the employment of the Panzer divisions, a very necessary component of all such formations was the Aufklärungs (reconnaissance) detachment. Their task was to probe ahead of the main body of armour and motorized infantry and artillery, providing information on the terrain and enemy dispositions; as versatile, highly mobile combat units they could also screen the flanks, or the rear during a retreat; and they were frequently thrown into action anywhere on the divisional front where reinforcements were needed quickly. In this way they served the same purpose as the cavalry of old.

Oberfeldwebel Richard Alber served in the same formation as Herbert Elsner – 23. Panzer Division – for the duration of the war. Initially he was with Kradschützen Bataillon 23 (Motorcycle Rifles Battalion 23). Such units, which were integral to the Panzer divisions before the outbreak of World War II and during the first three years of the conflict, were basically motorcycle-equipped 'mounted infantry', again echoing the part played by horsemen in a previous age of warfare. Their mission was to take lightly defended objectives quickly, to secure the forward areas and flanks of the division's advance, as well as to mount surprise attacks on the enemy.

In 1942 they started to receive more light armoured vehicles and cross-country vehicles such as the Schwimmwagen; but with the increasing vulnerability of such vehicles on the Eastern Front, and the duplication of roles with reconnaissance and Panzergrenadier units, it was decided in April 1943 to amalgamate the Kradschützen with the Aufklärungs Abteilungen within Panzer divisions. In 23. Panzer, this seems to have taken place in early October 1943.

By their very nature such units had to be at the 'tip of the spear' and were often the first to encounter the enemy. The hazards of service in an Aufklärungs Abteilung are underlined, in this case, by the award to Richard Alber of two grades of the Close Combat Clasp (*Nahkampfspange*), and the Wound Badge (*Verwundetenabzeichen*) in silver for either three or four wounds.

The uniform and equipment of Oberfeldwebel Alber illustrated on these pages were basically what he stood up in at the

end of the war. He was hospitalized for multiple shell fragment wounds when the war finished, and on discharge he returned home to find that everything he owned had been lost to Allied air raids; fortunately, the documents in this group, and the negatives for the photographs, were at his mother's residence, and had remained safe.

Oberfeldwebel Alber survived the war; but he had lost three brothers in the service of their country.

(**Left**) Alber, standing at far right, in his SdKfz 250 *neuer Art* half-track. This appears to be camouflaged in brown and green over the ochre-yellow factory finish. The marking on the left of the frontal plate cannot be made out, but the lower element may be 23. Panzer's arrow sign within a shield outline.

(Opposite page) Richard Alber, right, photographed wearing general service uniform outside an *Unteroffizier Heim* – an NCOs' Club. He displays the Iron Cross First Class but not the Close Combat Clasp, which might seem to date this snapshot to between mid-October and mid-November 1943; but this is an example of the care which must be taken to reconcile all known facts. We know from the award document for his second Close Combat Clasp that by March 1944, Alber still only held the rank of Unteroffizier. The shoulder straps in this photo have the complete *Tresse* edging of at least an Unterfeldwebel;

the two pin-on distinctions visible on the straps might be the single 'pip' of Feldwebel and his unit cypher, or the latter together with 'A' for Aufklärungs, if he was an Unterfeldwebel at this date. Either way, the photo clearly dates from later than 1 March 1944 – Alber simply is not wearing his Close Combat Clasp on this occasion.

(Right) A posed photograph, showing Richard Alber in the jacket illustrated below. He wears the Close Combat Clasp, but his rank is Feldwebel, which dates this photo to no earlier than spring 1944.

(Left) The complete uniform of Oberfeldwebel Alber gives us another rare opportunity to examine a uniform 'direct from the wearer', with all its personal modifications and effects. Alber was issued with the *feldgrau* assault artillery uniform which suited the exposed nature of the reconnaissance troops' front-line duties. The jacket displays all his awards, and also an interesting plaited cord – with a whistle? – passing from the upper right button inside the jacket.

The breast eagle is a standard BeVo pattern machine-woven in *feldgrau* on green, and has been reaffixed here – it was removed in 1945.

(Left & below) The shoulder straps are a personal adaptation. They are of the pre- or early-war type, showing bottle-green badge cloth and bright bullion NCO *Tresse*. They are very stiff, and would originally have been sewn-in parade straps; but they have been adapted later for wear in the field, by sewing on a tongue removed from another pair of straps, which was then sewed down to the shoulders of the jacket.

(Below) Although faded with age, the piping is in the bright *goldgelb* Waffenfarbe originally worn by the cavalry and later adopted by the Panzer Aufklärungs units. The collar patches are of the traditional Panzer design, but in field-grey wool – note the slight contrast between the shades of the collar itself and the patch bases. The stamped *Totenkopf* badges are the pattern with a triangular nose socket.

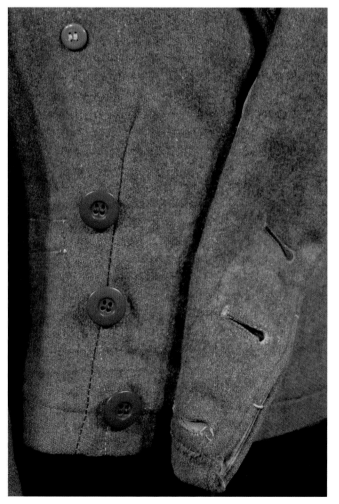

(**Above left & above**) The Alber field-grey *Panzerjacke* is fairly typical of mid- to late-war issue. It is stamped on the upper left lining with a Reichsbetriebsnummer, which were introduced late in 1942 for quality control reasons. Below this, in almost invisible white ink, are the usual size stamps, and the depot stamp '*F43*' for Frankfurt, 1943. Such markings are normally in black, but occasionally will be found in white; in this case they can be made out only by holding them up to the light at the exactly correct angle.

The lining is made of a 'silver-bronze' artificial silk, and is of the usual cut, with an open-topped, squared patch pocket on the inside right breast, and on the left a deep, curved-top pocket with a vertical opening for about the top half of the depth on the inner side. The belt hook tabs are not made of the lining fabric, but are separate webbing tapes which have been sewn on. The usual 'tunnel' for the waist adjustment tape runs across the small of the back.

(**Left**) The waist of the entire jacket has been shortened, bringing the front closure down from four buttons to three. Grey glass buttons are used throughout.

Oberfeldwebel Alber's trousers are another interesting example of private tailoring. While giving the appearance of a neat pair of *feldgrau* assault artillery issue, they are in fact tailored from a pair of straight M1936 general service uniform trousers – a clever imitation of the issue item which apparently was unavail-

able. That Richard Alber went to the trouble to acquire them is a reminder of how popular and fashionable the appearance of the armoured vehicle uniform was, among those entitled to wear it.

The slash pockets have had 'scallop-pointed' flaps and buttons added to imitate those of the *Panzerhose*, the legs have been

neatly taken in to give a narrower outline, and the bottoms have been elasticated for wearing bloused over ankle boots.

The rear of the waist retains the slightly higher cut, and the external buckled adjustment strap, of the general service trousers. Genuine issue assault gun trousers are identical in cut

to the black Panzer model, and feature an internal web waistbelt with a three-prong buckle (see page 67). The Alber trousers are stamped with the size and a maker's mark inside the front right hip on the white waistband.

(**Top**) The peaked cap obtained with the set is a private purchase *Schirmmütze* for NCO and enlisted ranks. It is piped in golden-yellow Waffenfarbe, and bears two stamped aluminium badges on the crown and band.

(**Left**) The good-quality lining is in a pale burgundy-coloured artificial silk, with a sweatshield impressed with the legend *'Die gute deutscher Mütze'* – 'The Good German Cap'. The front of the crown has been pinched together to make a sort of central 'lobe', giving it a desirable 'front-line veteran' appearance (as often also seen in photographs of Luftwaffe fighter pilots).

(**Above**) The most interesting feature is a sheet brass tradition badge for 23. Panzer Division, pinned at a slant to the left side of the band. Copying the division's vehicle sign, these badges were made in field workshops from available sheet metal, with two prongs soldered to the rear. They are seen in several photographs of members of 23. Panzer; and they were often worn together with a slightly larger version of the same design, fixed to a uniform-cloth patch which was then sewn to the upper right sleeve. There is ample photographic evidence that these insignia were worn during the war, especially the cap badge.

(Left) Thread loops have been sewn to the left breast to accommodate three of Alber's pin-back awards: the Iron Cross First Class, the Tank Battle Badge in Bronze, and the Wound Badge in silver. For the larger and heavier Close Combat Clasp, two small slashes have been cut and then reinforced with stitching (see below), to allow the horizontal pin actually to pass through the cloth of the jacket underneath the lining.

(Bottom left) The Iron Cross First Class is slightly vaulted, and is stamped 'L/11' – the manufacturer's code for the Wilhelm Deumer company in Lüdenscheid. The bronze Tank Battle Badge and silver Wound Badge are unmarked; the former has a resoldered catch, and little of the original bronze wash remains. The Close Combat Clasp in Silver, also unmarked, has a repaired hinge mount and a thin blued metal backing plate.

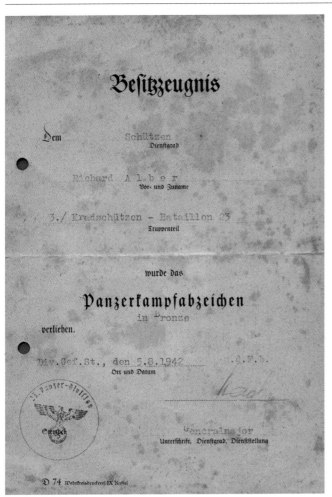

On this and the next page, Richard Alber's award documents are shown in chronological order.

(Left) The certificate for the *Panzerkampfabzeichen in Bronze* (Tank Battle Badge, in the version awarded to non-tank personnel who fought in armoured vehicles). Filled in with the name of Schütze Richard Alber of 3. Kompanie/Kradschützen Bataillon 23, the document is dated 5 August 1942. It is signed by the divisional commander Generalmajor Erwin Mack; just three weeks later, on 26 August, he would be killed by a Russian mortar attack while in the very front lines near Altud am Bakssan in the Caucasus.

(Below) The award certificate for the Iron Cross Second Class, dated 27 September 1942; Alber was still serving in the same rank and company. This sheet is signed by the next divisional commander, the *Ritterkreuzträger* Generalmajor Hans, Freiherr von Boineburg-Lengsfeld. This monocled Thuringian baron was perhaps the luckiest Panzer officer of the war: he survived multiple fractures when run over by a tank in Russia; he talked his way out of the potentially lethal dilemma of having prematurely arrested SS officers in Paris during the July 1944 'bomb plot', in which he was implicated; and finally, he had his court martial – for disobeying Hitler's orders to blow up the Seine bridges and defend Paris to the last – aborted by the end of the war. He led 23. Panzer Division from 26 August to 28 December 1942.

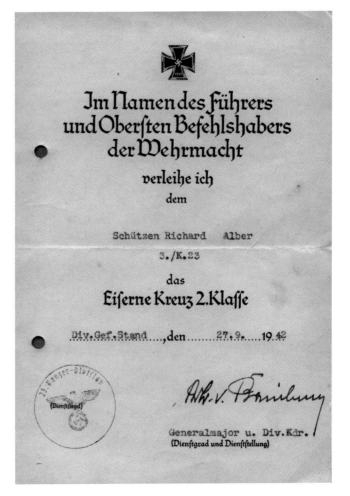

(Left) On 9 October 1943, Unteroffizier Alber of 4. Kompanie/Panzer Aufklärungs Abteilung 23 was awarded the Iron Cross First Class. The award document is signed personally by Generalleutnant Nikolaus von Vormann, another Knight's Cross holder, who was divisional commander between 28 December 1942 and 25 October 1943.

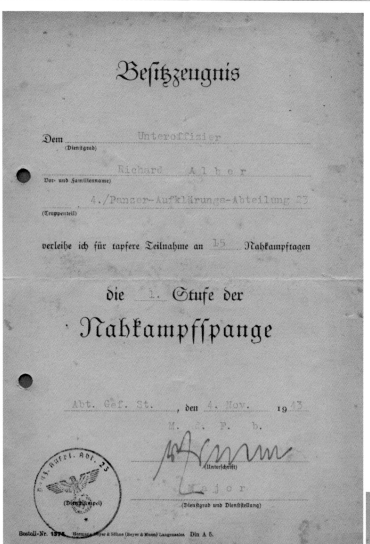

The Close Combat Clasp *(Nahkampfspange)* was instituted by Hitler on 25 November 1942, to recognize those veterans of infantry combat – in any relevant arm of service – who had far surpassed the requirements for the award of the original Infantry Assault Badge. The new clasp was to be awarded to officers and men who had repeatedly taken part in close-quarter combat, unsupported by armoured vehicles. It was to be awarded in three progressive classes: bronze, silver and gold. The eligibility requirement for the bronze clasp was 15 days of close combat (or 10 days, if wounded); for the silver, 30 days (or 20, if wounded); and for the gold, 50 days (or 40, if wounded). When the clasp was instituted it could be awarded retrospectively for service since June 1941, and a notional ratio equating length of front-line service to combat days was devised: 8 months' service was counted as 5 combat days, 12 months' as 10 days, and 15 months' as 15 days.

(Above) On 4 November 1943, Unteroffizier Richard Alber of 4./Pz.Aufkl.Abt. 23 was awarded the *Nahkampfspange '1. Stufe'* (bronze) for 15 days of close quarter combat. The document is signed by Major von Einem of the division's Panzerjäger Abteilung 128, during a period when he held dual command.

(Right) On 1 March 1944, Unteroffizier Alber – still with 4.Kompanie – was awarded the silver clasp, '2. Stufe', for 30 days of close quarter fighting. This document is signed by Major Hoppe, commander of Panzer Aufklärungs Abteilung 23.

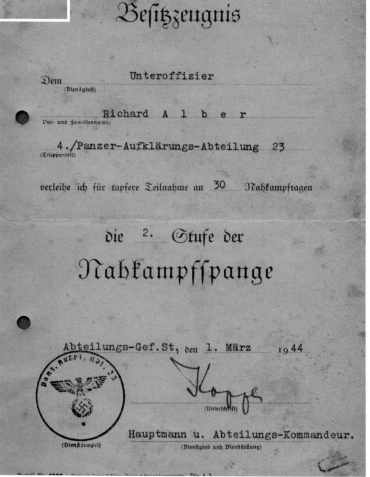

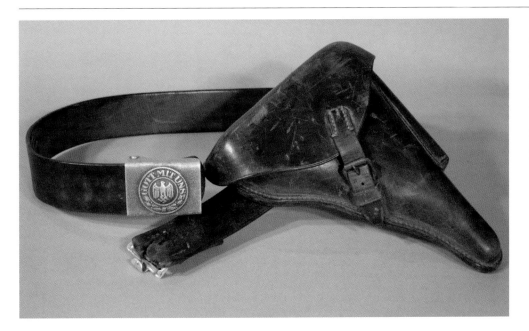

(Left & below) Among the other mementoes of Alber's service are this belt, and a hard-shell pistol holster in brown leather for a P08 Luger. The holster is a re-issue item that had originally been used in World War I. There is an impress of the maker in Ulm, the date '*1913*', and a Bekleidungsampt ink stamp for 1913.

(Right) The belt is an absolutely standard piece, but has a fascinating story to tell. The injuries that put Oberfeldwebel Alber in hospital at the end of World War II were several fragment wounds: one to the head, a splinter in his back (evidenced by a small hole in the back of his *Panzerjacke*), and another piece which was stopped by the clasp on his belt. There is a significant hole, and the internal section of the clip is bent out of shape by the strike. It appears that this prevented a serious stomach wound, as the hole did not penetrate the overlapping end of the belt behind.

(Left) Finally, there is Alber's issue wristwatch. German issue watches were made by many different European makers, some still in business today. This steel-cased timepiece is made by the Record Watch Co. of Geneva, Switzerland, and carries a serial number between a capital '*D*' and '*H*' to signify 'Deutsches Heer', German Army.

MISCELLANEOUS ITEMS

Instructional tank models

During the war a series of 1:20 scale models of both German and Allied tanks was made as training aids for the German Army. It appears that two separate companies manufactured these; one, an engineering firm in Berlin, produced models with flat tracks, while a toy company made them with very intricate tracks. The models were generally made of wood, and had moving parts such as wheels, machine guns, turrets and cannon. Glued to the underside was a printed card giving basic specification data for the subject tank. It is thought that these models were supplied to organizations such as tank and anti-tank training schools. They naturally proved to be a popular souvenir for Allied soldiers after the war, but are quite rare today – understandably, most were subsequently played with, to the point of destruction, by small boys.

(Left & below) This beautiful hand-made wooden model PzKw VI Tiger Ausf E measures 31cm long (without gun) X 18cm wide X 13cm high – just over 12in X 7in X 5in. Moving parts include the turret, 8.8cm gun, hull machine gun and driver's vision plate. The bottom of the data sheet fixed to the belly states that it was provided by the Inspectorate of Armoured Troops.

(Bottom left) This M4A1 Sherman is typical of the models made by the toy manufacturer. Apart from the guns and turret, the intricately made tracks are also movable.

(Left) Model of PzKw V Panther Ausf G.

(Right) Model of PzKw IV Ausf F2. The stencilled notice on the side reminds users that this is a service item and that misuse is a punishable offence – there must have been many Panzer soldiers who thought of small sons, brothers or nephews as soon as they saw these models.

(Left) Model of StuG III Ausf G assault gun. Note the long wooden side rails: these were for mounting cardboard miniatures of the protective sheet metal side skirts or 'Schürzen', which are missing from this model.

(Right) Now missing its tracks, a model of the Soviet T-34/76, complete with the wooden box in which it was sent home to New York in 1945 by Lt Rakowski of the US Army's 19th Tank Battalion.

During the war the famous ceramic company of Goebel made a series of 1:100 scale models in porcelain for use by the German armed forces. It is thought that 20 different models were made altogether, covering various German and Allied tanks and other armoured vehicles. The models were used for map board presentations, silhouette identification, and troop training in 'sand boxes' – when trainees practised using weapon sights and drivers' vision devices lined up on indoor miniature dioramas.

On the underside all these models bore the company logo (the letters 'WG', for the founder Wihelm Goebel, surmounted by a crown), and the name – sometimes abbreviated – of the vehicle. Today these models are considered quite rare, since (being of hollow porcelain) many naturally did not survive. A limited number of examples were also made in 1:33 scale; surviving examples of these are believed to be exceptionally rare.

(Top) Ten Goebel models, with a 50 Euro-cents coin for scale – Allied types in the back row, German in the front.

(Above) Undersides of Tiger and StuG models, showing imprinted names and company logo.

(Left) This article in a wartime issue of *Signal* magazine shows what may be a Goebel model used for sandbox training of anti-tank gun crews.

This highly detailed 1:18 scale model of a Sturmgeschütz III Ausf B is not a training aid but a presentation gift. Although the mark of StuG shown dated from 1940, the model was presented in the closing stages of the war to Unteroffizier Hermann Böhl of 3. Batterie/Sturmgeschütz Brigade 191 by his commanding officer, who was apparently a Ritterkreuzträger. It was in congratulation for an individual defensive action, without supporting infantry, that saw seven Soviet tanks destroyed and infantry attacks repelled. Bohl was commissioned in the rank of Leutnant and proposed for higher awards, but as the war was in its last days these were never made.

(Left) The model was made from steel, probably in a brigade workshop, and weighs nearly 5kg (11 pounds). This superb example of miniature metalwork has a traversable gun, opening top hatches, individually sprung wheels and individually linked tracks. The General Assault Badge is shown here for scale.

(Above) Unteroffizier Bohl seen in the cupola of a StuG III Ausf G in Italy in summer 1944; note the streak-and-dot camouflage painting of the side skirts, and the number '222'. Sturmgeschütz Abteilung (later Brigade) 191 fought in France in 1940; the Balkans, then central Russia in 1941; at Rostov and Kursk in 1942–43; in Italy, and then on the Eastern Front again in 1944–45.

(Right) Unteroffizier Böhl started the war in a veterinary company, but transferred to the Sturmgeschütze after the 1940 French campaign. He was awarded Iron Cross Second Class, General Assault Badge *II. Stufe* for 25 assaults, the Wound Badges in black and silver, and the *Ostmedaille*. Captured by the Soviets, he did not return home until 1949. He is seen here in 1944 wearing the assault artillery jacket with red-piped Panzer-style collar patches. Note the cord from his top right button, and see Ofw Alber's jacket on page 95.

Instruction manuals

In 1943 the Oberkommando der Wehrmacht (Armed Forces High Command) and the Inspectorate of Armoured Troops decided that a general manual was required for soldiers as an introduction to the new PzKw VI Tiger tank. The officer in charge, Leutnant von Glatter-Goetz, decided that it would be more readily accessible to the soldiers, and more likely to hold their attention, if it were designed using cartoon drawings and some humour in the text.

(Above) The result was a small paperback-sized book of 92 pages with a stiff card cover, the *Tigerfibel* or 'Tiger Primer ... for platoon commanders and Tiger crews'. Its front cover boast that readers would 'get the point so quickly' was well founded; the format proved so popular and effective that it would be copied in several more manuals. (Indeed, its ancestry can be made out in a number of military manuals produced since World War II.)

(Right) Inside the back cover was a small pocket containing range and targeting sheets for the five most common Allied tanks, showing the correct 'sight picture' for the 8.8cm KwK 36 main gun; two larger identification and data posters of various Allied armoured vehicles; and a targeting fold-out showing 'soft points' of various enemy tanks.

(Left) On page 54 the manual suggested that soldiers treat the 8.8cm ammunition as they would treat a lady, protecting the shells from sunshine and rain, guarding them against accidental damage, and not trying to take them apart. The recognition colours of the different types of round are noted: armour-piercing *Panzergranate 39*, black with white tip, and tungsten-cored *Panzergranate 40*, black; chemical *HL-granate*, grey; and high explosive *Sprenggranate*, yellow. The 'moral' may be roughly translated thus: 'Whether blonde, brunette or grey - make as much fuss of her as you would of your bride. The result will be sensational: one touch of your finger, and she'll catch fire!'

(Left) After the success of the *Tigerfibel* it was decided to use the same approach to tackle another growing problem: that of teaching infantrymen to defend themselves against tanks. In mid-1944 the *Panzerknacker* manual appeared ('Tank-Cracker', as in 'nut-cracker'). The cover showed a soldier using an old-fashioned nut-cracker to crush a Soviet tank. The 24-page soft-cover booklet was an immediate success; a separate but identical version was produced for Luftwaffe ground troops.

(Above) Although 'tank-cracker' was originally the nickname for a hazardous hand-placed magnetic shaped charge, and the manual illustrated various methods for disabling tanks in the absence of conventional anti-armour weapons, it also showed the very latest equipment: the *Panzerfaust* disposable anti-tank rocket launcher, and the reloadable 8.8cm *Panzerschreck* based on US bazookas captured from the Red Army. The manual was produced in conjunction with a training film *Manner Gegen Panzer* ('Men Against Tanks'). These drawings warn against the weapons' backblast.

(Above & right) A couple of months later the OKW published the *Panther-Fibel* or 'Panther Primer', again employing cartoons, humour, mottoes and rhymes to hammer home the essentials for the crews of the PzKw V. This booklet had a stiff card cover and printing in several colours. This page shows the Panther tank as a gift brought by saints and angels to the grateful Panzer trooper, and urges him to 'Learn with Pleasure!' how to get the most out of his hard-hitting new pet.

(**Left & below**) Another manual that appeared in 1944 was a new 40-page paperback entitled *Panzer Helfen Dir!* ('Armour Helps You!'). Again using language any soldier could understand, together with catoons, it was intended to teach infantrymen the fundamentals of how best to work with armour – here, what tasks and protection could reasonably be expected of the different types of light armoured vehicle, and what could not.

(**Left & below**) In 1944 a civilian manual was also produced, to inspire the general public and educate them about their tank troops. Priced at 90 Reichspfennigs, *Die Panzertruppen* was a paperback-sized booklet of 128 pages. Its chapters included a brief history of the Panzertruppe, sectional diagrams explaining how tanks worked, photos of tanks in action, and a large identification section on German and Allied tanks and their basic specification data.

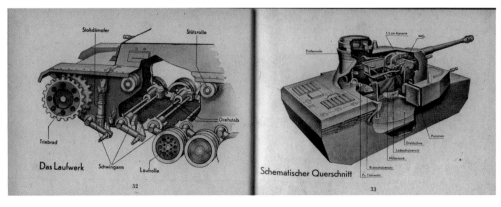

Trophies and souvenirs

(Left) In the pre-war Army it was not unusual for Panzer soldiers to be presented with trophies for various achievements, or Christmas gifts when they were away from home. Shown here are various items that would be presented on such occasions.

The plaque, left, shows PzKw I light tanks; note the use of signalling flags – radios were not yet fitted to any but command vehicles. The inscription reads *Für gute Leistungen/als Fahrer/8. Pz Rgt.1 16.12.37* – 'For good performance as a driver, 8. Kompanie, Panzer Regiment 1, 16 December 1937'. Next to this is a typical 'heroic soldier' bust, showing a tank crewman wearing the *Schutzmütze*. Foreground is a silvered metal model of a PzKw I, also on a polished stone base; this sort of piece was most likely to be found on an officer's desk.

(Right) Two more practical gifts. The bakelite cigarette case has an inset commemoration of time spent on the *Panzertruppenschule/ Techn. Lehrgänge/1938* ('Tank Troops School Technical Course'). At the front is a soldier's penknife with an inlaid inscription *Panzer-Abwehr Abteilung 37/ Weihnachten 1938* ('Anti-Tank Battalion 37/ Christmas 1938').

(Left) This pewter plate commemorates a soldier's service with 3. Kompanie/Panzer Abwehr Abteilung 20 between October 1936 and May 1937. The centre bears a disc showing the unit badge, a fist crushing an old Renault FT-17 tank. At right is a large commemorative stamp bearing the same motif and the unit designation. All unit canteens sold a number of ready-made souvenir and gift items inscribed to the particular unit.

(Below) Another popular memento was the official photo album. These were presented to soldiers at the end of their compulsory military service, and canteens always held a stock of other albums with suitable designs on the covers. The official albums usually contained several pages showing portraits of leading figures such as the Führer and the Chief of the Army General Staff, as well as a brief illustrated history of the German Army. Additional pages referred to the soldier's particular unit, usually including both its history and relevant group photos.

Photographs

In a period when black-and-white photographs were the norm, hand-tinted coloured prints were a popular way of bringing a special picture to life.

(Left) Not all photographs were intended for albums. The locket shown on the left, with a hand-coloured print of a young Panzer soldier wearing the *Schutzmütze* and a first-pattern jacket, has on the back a second tinted image of the same individual as a young member of the Hitler Youth. The oval print on the right, mounted on a metal backing under clear celluloid, shows a young Panzerschütze in front-line mode, wearing the field cap and a second-pattern *Panzerjacke* over a roll-neck sweater.

(Right) This Panzerjäger Oberfeldwebel wears the field-grey assault artillery jacket with pink-piped black Panzer collar patches complete with *Totenkopf* badges. The shoulder straps appear to carry the 'P' cypher for Panzerjäger. He displays the Close Combat Clasp (which dates the photograph to 1943 at the earliest), the General Assault Badge and Iron Cross First Class.

(Left) Here a Sturmartillerie officer wears the complete *feldgrau* armoured vehicle uniform. Note the general service collar *Litzen* with artillery-red 'lights', dating this picture to after the withdrawal of the Panzer-style collar patches at the beginning of 1943. His decorations are the Iron Cross First Class, Wound Badge, and Tank Battle Badge; the familiar pair of ribbons in his buttonhole are the Iron Cross Second Class and the *Winterschlacht im Osten 1941/42* medal. He has tucked under his arm the officer's version of the M1943 cap with silver crown piping, and insignia machine-woven on a single T-shaped backing.

(Below) This very 'new-looking' Panzer Leutnant wears no awards but an immaculate uniform; everything looks fresh and clean, even his leather belt and gloves. The jacket is of the second pattern, with a quite pronounced pointed shape to the collar. His peaked cap is the officer's *Feldmütze alter Art* ('old-style field cap'), without chin cords and with flat, machine-woven BeVo insignia; the very glossy peak with a raised, pressed edge recalls that of the *'Perküro'* cap illustrated on page 75.

(Right) This Feldwebel of Panzerjäger Abteilung 24 – identified by the cypher and numerals on his shoulder straps – wears the black Panzer uniform, and would have rose-pink Waffenfarbe piping on his insignia. The most remarkable detail is the individual use of the *'Braunschweiger'* (Brunswick) shape of death's-head badge on the collar patches, instead of the issue *'Danziger'* pattern. This was a strictly personal touch, and only rarely observed.

(Right) This extremely rare photograph shows a young Obergefreiter (senior private) of the Panzerkorps 'Feldherrnhalle' on the day he was awarded the Iron Cross Second Class – the only occasion on which the cross itself was ever displayed on its suspension ribbon. On the left cuff of his third-pattern jacket is the 'Feldherrnhalle' cuff title illustrated on page 58; but he does not wear the special shoulder strap cyphers, which were rarely seen on the uniforms of enlisted personnel. Note the light grey-on-black breast eagle; the silver-grey double chevron of his rank, worn on the left sleeve only; the *Panzerkampfabzeichen*, and the Wound Badge in black; and his black Panzer M1943 cap with the insignia machine-woven on a black backing.

(**Left**) Officers of Sturmgeschütz Brigade 341 in Normandy, summer 1944. The man on the left wears standard field-grey assault artillery vehicle uniform with the old sidecap. On the right, with his M1943 cap swathed in mosquito veiling, is Hauptmann Gerhard Pazur, who wears a modified Panzer drill uniform of reed-green herringbone twill, with the thin jacket tucked inside the trousers. He has had a large map pocket added to the left breast, with a zipped top opening, indicating that this is a first-pattern jacket; the second pattern was manufactured with an external map pocket. Pazur wears full insignia on this lightweight jacket, and his shirt collar is folded down outside the closed jacket collar. Hauptmann Pazur was killed at Brecey in Normandy on 31 July 1944.

(**Below**) Two handsome young Panzer soldiers pose for the camera. The use of non-regulation shirts is quite often seen. The use of non-regulation shirts is quite often seen and it appears that pinstripe and white shirts were especially fashionable. The Unteroffizier's jacket has a very large collar – such variations between makers was not uncommon. He displays the *Ostmedaille* ribbon, and on his left sleeve the Demjansk Shield. This was awarded in April 1943 to commemorate the prolonged defence of that encircled town by units of II Armeekorps.

(**Above**) A relaxed snapshot of Hauptmann Eric Schippert, left, with his adjutant in 1944. Schippert was the commanding officer of schwere Panzerjäger Abteilung 519 (Heavy Anti-Tank Battalion 519); such units were normally equipped with either the Nashorn – an 8.8cm tank-hunter with an open superstructure built on the PzKw IV hull – or the formidable fully enclosed and heavily armoured 8.8cm Jagdpanther. Schippert was a holder of the German Cross in Gold, displayed here on his field-grey assault artillery jacket along with his Iron Cross First Class, black Wound Badge, and – interestingly – the Infantry Assault Badge. The use of the black Panzer M1943 cap with *feldgrau* uniform is striking. It is puzzling that the commanding officer wears Panzer-type collar patches, while his adjutant, and the medic behind the half-track, have artillery *Litzen*.

(Above) A popular souvenir of a Panzer soldier's service, particularly pre-war, was the Kompanie group photo. This particular group were photographed outside their Kaserne in 1938, all wearing the Panzer *Schutzmütze* and the first-pattern *Panzerjacke*. The photo is mounted on a special backing card with elaborate Panzer motifs.

(Inset above) Note the little son of the Kompanie Spiess wearing a miniature copy of his father's uniform right down to the Hauptfeldwebel's 'piston rings' on the sleeves and a marksmanship lanyard on the right shoulder. The officers flanking him wear their silver brocade full dress belts for this occasion.

(Above) Another proud son, almost engulfed by his father's *Schutzmütze* and jacket. Note the Leutnant's shoulder straps, and the officer's-quality insignia on the beret.

(Right) In a similar image, Hauptmann Stöckl of 2. Kompanie/Panzer Regiment 25 poses on a PzKw I with his little boy at Erlangen in 1938; again, the toddler has been fitted out with a complete miniature uniform.

Personal snapshots sometimes show the daughters, sisters or sweethearts of Panzer soldiers posing in the borrowed glory of their glamorous uniforms.

(Right) This bold Fraulein appears to fit the Unteroffizier's *Schirmmütze* and uniform jacket admirably.

(Above) This must surely be a girlfriend; she appears to wear a complete first-pattern *Panzer-anzug*, from shirt and tie out-wards. The snapshot gives us a rare opportunity to see a Panzer Pioniere ensemble, with black-and-white twist piping on the collar and patches of the jacket.

(Right) Perhaps a precious memento of a very rare wartime Christmas leave? This daughter is obviously proud of her Unteroffizier father's field cap and third-pattern jacket; as in the photo above, it is worn com-plete with the aluminium plaited cord marksmanship lanyard on the shoulder.

Portraits

(**Right**) Often a painting can give valuable details about a uniform and the man who wore it. This example, found at a 'flea market' in southern Germany, very accurately shows a young Offizieranwärter or officer candidate of the Sturmartillerie, and is dated 1944. The subject's name on the rear of the frame is Gottfried Krietsch, together with the name of an artist from Leipzig. A search of the German war graves registration brings up an Unteroffizier by this name, killed at the age of 20 on 27 November 1943 near Bobruisk in Belarus. The soldier was born in Bautzen, some 80 miles west of Leipzig. A posthumous portrait commissioned by the family, perhaps? – the rather sombre expression would be plausible.

The young man's substantive rank is Unteroffizier, and he wears the field-grey armoured artillery vehicle tunic with the mid-war *Litzen* collar patches, on a dark green base piped in artillery red. On his red-piped, dark green shoulder straps are the *Tresse* edging of this rank, and double *Tresse* loops identifying an aspirant officer. He displays both classes of the Iron Cross as well as the General Assault Badge.

(**Left**) This rather grandly framed oil portrait shows a veteran Panzer Unteroffizier who is, again, an aspirant officer. The subject's name is not known, but he wears the second-pattern *Panzerjacke*, with shoulder straps bearing the number '*118*'. There was a Panzer Abteilung 118 that was raised in late September 1943 and served with the 18. Panzer Division. It was destroyed in June 1944 on the central sector of the Eastern Front during the collapse of Army Group Centre in the face of the massive Soviet summer offensive, Operation 'Bagration'; but it was subsequently re-raised, although as a Sturmgeschütz unit, in late 1944.

This NCO wears the ribbons of the War Service Cross and the Iron Cross Second Class on his lapel, as well as the silver Tank Battle Badge and silver Wound Badge on his left breast. As in the photographs on pages 95 and 107, he wears a plaited cord – not a marksmanship lanyard – from his right shoulder and apparently passing inside the jacket to the internal pocket.

(Left) This fine example of a hand-coloured portrait photograph shows a young Panzer soldier probably in late 1938. He is wearing the piped first-pattern Panzer jacket, identified by the square cut of the collar and the lack of buttons on the upper right breast or buttonholes on the left lapel. The marksmanship lanyard, grade 1, is of the first pattern; the shield set on the top 'flounder' of the cord was replaced in January 1939 with a more elaborate design surrounded by a wreath, dating this portrait to before that time. On his chest he wears what appears to be the 13 March 1938 Medal commemorating the return of Austria to the Reich, although the centre of the ribbon should be bright red.

(Right) This very large pastel portrait portrays an Unteroffizier of Panzerjäger wearing the M1935 *Waffenrock* and the *Schirmmütze* with the pink distinctions for 'Schnelle Truppen'. Apart from the 'P' cyphers on the shoulder straps this is also the cap and tunic issued to all Panzer soldiers. Black cloth loops around the straps possibly hide any unit designation; this, and the ribbon of the Iron Cross Second Class in his buttonhole, date the portrait after the outbreak of World War II. The ribbon bar on his breast is for service on the Westwall in 1939–40. The cut of this tunic and the peaked cap would indicate privately tailored rather than issue items, the prerogative of those NCOs who could afford it. On the outbreak of war manufacture of this parade and walking-out dress tunic was suspended for the duration, and most of those already held were limited thereafter to wear for occasional formal functions.

Paybooks

The *Soldbuch* was the soldier's personal identity book, and was to be carried at all times. It contained all relevant information about his day-to-day service – his pay, the uniforms and equipment issued to him the units he served in, when he went on leave, his next of kin, and many other minutiae. In one small pocketbook it catalogued his whole official existence as a soldier. Because the *Soldbuch* was always carried and was of fairly flimsy construction, surviving examples will often be found to show heavy wear and tear, and have frequently been repaired – which gives them a touch of character.

With the right reference sources and some patient detective work, it is possible to find out a lot about a soldier's career from his paybook. The example illustrated on this page belonged to a Panzer soldier named Willi Troost.

(Left) Opposite the photo on the first page Troost's promotions are shown, from Gefreiter in October 1935, to Feldwebel in September 1943, and Oberfeldwebel in April 1945. The paper tag above his picture, dated 10 November 1944, states that he is assigned to Panzer Abteilung 302 (Fkl) – for Funklenk, 'radio control' – as a specialist with radio-controlled weapons. Troost in fact finished the war with Sturmgeschütz Abteilung 400, and was captured by the British, who put him to work as an electrician. Troost's awards included the War Service Cross in both classes, the Tank Battle Badge in silver and the Wound Badge in black.

Units with the suffix 'Fkl' operated radio-controlled tracked armoured vehicles that could deliver a charge to a target for remote-controlled demolition; Troost served with both Pz Abt (Fkl) 300 and later 302. The best-known equipment of this type was the little SdKfz 303 Goliath, a knee-high box on tracks, which carried a charge of 183lb of TNT and was controlled down a 2,000m cable; the initial Goliath E was unveiled at Kursk in July 1943.

However, Troost is more likely to have operated the SdKfz 301 Funklenkpanzer BIV. This much larger vehicle was driven on the approach march by a driver, who then dismounted and sent it forward under radio control,

triggering the release of an enormous 1,212lb charge; theoretically he then brought it back to German lines, but in fact most were destroyed by the explosion of their own charges. The SdKfz 301 was sometimes used in conjunction with Tiger tank units.

(Right) Apart from the issue to Willi Troost of several pistols, noted on page 8a, there is a very complete entry on page 8c for the issue in September 1943 of an MP40 machine pistol. This notes the gun number, 3886m, as well as two magazine pouches, six magazines and a magazine loading tool. There is also a rare entry for a *Dienstarmbanduhr* or service wristwatch, on 1 April 1944.

(Left) Pages 12 & 13 show all hospitalizations. Each type of injury was given a number, e.g. 35a for gunshot wounds; shell fragment injuries were 31b – as shown here. Troost was in Motorized Field Hospital 2/610 (Army Group South) on 28 June 1942. He arrived at a Reserve Hospital at Przemysl, Poland, 12 days later, and was transferred to a hospital in Bad Griesbach, Germany, on 14 July. On 21 October his *Soldbuch* was marked 'K.V.' for Kriegsverwendungsfähig – fit for active service.

(Top right) The *Soldbuch* and military driver's licence shown on this page were issued to Obergefreiter Benedikt Jäger. It appears that he started his career in 1939 as an infantryman, with 4./Infantry Replacement Battalion 61, before transferring to the artillery in 1942, becoming a member of Assault Gun Replacement Battalion 300. In 1944 he went to Sturmgeschütz Brigade 279, which was serving on the Russian Front; but was then consecutively transferred to Sturmgeschütz Ersatz Abteilung 500, and finally to Sturmgesch. Ers. Abt. 400 in peaceful Denmark.

It would seem that the fortunate Obergefreiter Jäger held some training position, since his only award was the War Service Cross Second Class with Swords. His paybook also reveals that, unlike front-line crewmen, he did not receive a pistol but was issued a Mauser 98k rifle – and even this was later replaced with a captured Polish Radom rifle.

An interesting typewritten entry from November 1942 is pasted in the medical examinations section (page 14), noting that after undergoing X-ray treatment and blood tests Jäger was declared unsuitable for tropical service because of a blood deficiency.

Note that the binding of his *Soldbuch* has been sewn with cotton thread to prevent the pages from falling out.

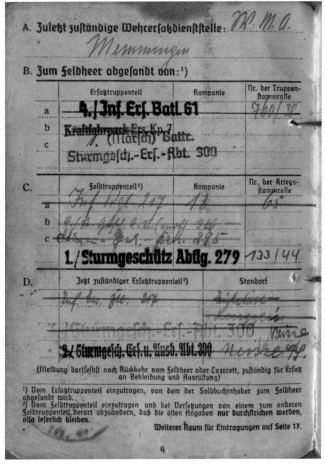

(Below) A clean example of a document which is rarely found with the *Soldbuch* – the owner's matching military driver's licence. Signed by Jäger's Hauptmann, this is a 2nd Class licence (motor cars), entitling him to drive Verbrennungsmaschinen – literally, vehicles with a combustion engine. This bears the same photograph of Jäger wearing the field-grey assault artillery jacket, with red-piped, field-grey, Panzer-style collar patches, but displaying neither *Totenkopf* badges nor *Litzen*. This is interesting, since the licence, issued when Jäger was with Sturmgeschütz Ersatz Abteilung 300, is clearly dated 21 October 1942, and thus predates the official order of January 1943 forbidding wear of the death's-heads by non-tank or anti-tank personnel. In the photo Jäger also wears the field-grey enlisted ranks' shoulder straps with a blank loop covering any unit designation.

(Above) Page 4 has a list of units the bearer has served in. If the page gets filled up, as is often the case, then there is more space to continue the list on page 17 – which is where we find the entry for Benedikt Jäger's final assignment to Assault Gun Replacement Battalion 400 on occupation duties in Denmark.

Identification tags

Soldiers in most belligerent armies of World War II wore some form of identification tags, both while they were alive and, if they fell, after their death. The German *Erkennungsmarke* was an oval plaque of either zinc or thin steel measuring 7cm X 5cm (roughly, 2¾ X 2 inches). There were holes punched through at the top and the bottom to allow for suspension around the neck. There were also three rectangular perforations across the centre. The tag was stamped with identical information on both top and bottom halves. Should the wearer be killed, the tag was broken in two at the perforations; the free half was returned to the unit for its records, and the other half was left around the neck for subsequent identification of the body.

Unlike both American and British tags or discs, the German type did not carry the name of the recipient. The information stamped into the tag generally followed a prescribed layout. There was the wearer's unit designation (always in an abbreviated form); the individual's number on that unit's nominal roll (*Stammroll*); and finally his blood group (*Blutgruppe*). Various placements of these elements can be found on surviving tags, and they are stamped into the metal with differing levels of skill. Some tags will have been provided to a new recruit at the depot, while others were made by headquarters units in the field with a hand stamping kit.

Tags were officially to be suspended around the neck on an 80cm (31½in) long cord; however, during the war it became apparent that the bodies of some servicemen (such as airmen and tank crews, particularly) were likely to have sustained damage – particularly from burning – which separated the tag from the body. For this reason a metal suspension chain was introduced for these categories of servicemen in August 1942. The chain was also 80cm long, and had a seamless join.

It is interesting to note that several of the tags illustrated on the following pages were found in a dump at the site of a former Soviet camp for German prisoners-of-war. It appears that the tags meant nothing to the Russians – unlike the *Soldbuch* or other identity papers, which they preserved, these tags were simply discarded *en masse*.

(**Below**) Shown at left is a rare example of a Panzer soldier's *Erkennungsmarke* with the fireproof chain introduced in August 1942. It is unissued. It is not known if these chained tags were provided in any great numbers, but they are exceptionally rare in present-day collections.

On the right is a standard *Erkennungsmarke* for a member of the 8th Company, Tank Regiment 'Großdeutschland' – '8./ PANZ. RGT. G.D.'. The Stammroll number '37' is stamped below this abbreviated designation; and blood group 'B' is stamped at the right side of both upper and lower halves. The tag is suspended on a typical issue cord.

(Right) This rare Panzer tag with chain was worn until the end of the war by Oberfeldwebel Herbert Mergans, who ended the war as a *Funkmeister* (Radio Sergeant) in the Stabskompanie of schwere Panzer Abteilung 507.

Heavy Tank Battalion 507 was raised in September 1943; the unit sign painted on some of its tanks was a shield shape enclosing the figure of a black-smith forging a sword on an anvil. Commanded by Major Erich Schmidt and equipped with the PzKw VI Tiger Ausf E ('Tiger I'), it first saw combat in March 1944 on the Eastern Front, in defensive battles around Tarnopol, Vitebsk and on the Narev river. Hauptmann Fritz Schöck took over comm-

mand in August 1944. In February 1945 the battalion was re-equipped with the König-stiger (King Tiger or 'Tiger II'), before returning to the Eastern Front, where it ended the war fighting in Czechoslovakia. After losing all their tanks in action the survivors moved westwards in an attempt to reach the advancing US forces, but they were cut off and captured by the Red Army.

None of this dramatic history can be discovered simply by examining this *Erkennungsmarke* – the research depends on the *Soldbuch*. Soldiers often contin-ued to carry the first tag that they had been issued by their original inducting unit for sev-eral years; this example was issued to Herbert Mergans in

March 1940, but he continued to wear it until his capture in 1945. It carries the abbreviation *ST.PZ.ABW.ERS.ABT. 189*, which indicates the Stabskom-panie of Panzer Abwehr Ersatz

Abteilung 189 – 'HQ Company/ Anti-Tank Replacement Batta-lion 189'. Mergans' *Stamroll* number was '48', and his blood group 'A/B'.

(Below) The first two pages of Herbert Mergans' *Soldbuch*. Note that his initial unit, blood type and roll number were recorded on the first right hand page. Mergans' promotions are listed from Gefreiter in May 1941, to Obergefreiter in March 1942, Unteroffizier in October 1942 and 'Unteroffizier im Funkmeis-

terdienst' in December 1944, culminating in Oberfeldwebel Funkmeister in April 1945. At the top right corner of his photo-graph on the inside cover – which shows him as an Un-teroffizier or Unterfelwebel – the partial stamp of s.Pz.Abt. 507 can just be made out.

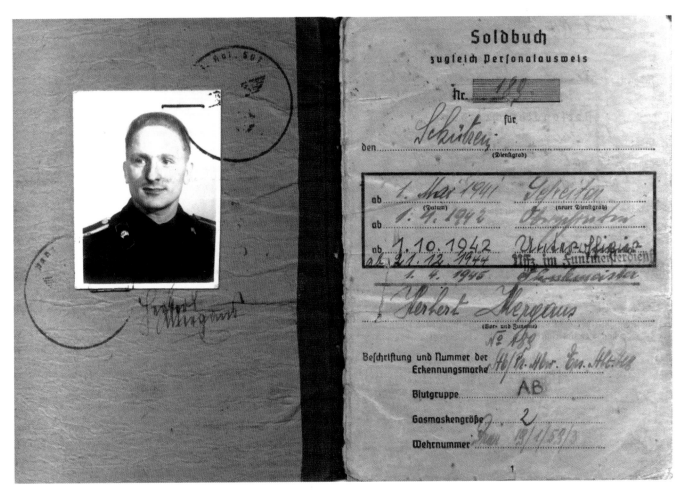

(Right) This disc carries the abbreviation 'ST.KP./PZ.AUFKL. ERS.U.AUSB.ABT. 55', for Stabskompanie/Panzer Aufklärungs Ersatz und Ausbildungs Abteilung 55 – 'HQ Company/ Armoured Reconnaissance Replacement and Training Battalion 55.' This unit was reorganized and redesignated in April 1943 as Panzer Aufklärungs Abteilung 103, serving as part of the re-formed 3. Panzergrenadier Division after the original formation had been wiped out at Stalingrad. Headquarters elements of reconnaissance battalions often had heavy support weapons, and the Stabskompanie of Pz.Aufkl.Abt. 103 included StuG III assault guns. This division went on to fight in Italy in 1943–44, and in France and the Ardennes before surrendering in the Ruhr Pocket in 1945. This soldier's number on the unit nominal roll was '876' and his blood group 'B'.

(Right) Aluminium tag from a possibly unfortunate member of Infantry Anti-Tank Company 270 – such companies were later absorbed into Panzerjäger units. The abbreviation is 'INF.PANZ. ABW.KP. 270'. The fate of the soldier listed on the nominal roll as '120' is unknown. Ironically enough, his tag bears no blood group stamp.

(Right) Soldier number '228', whose blood group was 'A', was serving with '2./Pz.Aufkl.Abt. 5' – '2nd Company/Armoured Reconnaissance Battalion 5'. This Panzer Aufklärungs Abteilung was integral to 5. Panzer Division, fighting exclusively on the Eastern Front from 1941. The tag is made out of aluminium.

Remembrance cards

Remembrance cards, which were distributed among the relatives and friends of fallen soldiers as a commemoration of their loss, are an increasingly popular subject for militaria collectors. This is not just for the sake of the uniform and insignia evidence which their portrait photographs provide, but also because they are 'capsules' which assist more detailed research into the careers of individuals. They contain details of a soldier's date of birth, date of death, rank, arm of service, and the general area where he was killed. For obvious wartime security reasons they do not give specifics of a man's unit, but they are an important foundation upon which further detective work can be based.

Records of the dead and their possible resting places can be found at the website of the Volksbund Deutsche Kriegsgräberfürsorge (German Wargraves Organization) at *www.volksbund.de*. This is a private humanitarian organization that relies on donations to maintain the resting places of millions of soldiers in 842 cemeteries across 44 countries.

In a more human sense, of course, these *memento mori* cards are a lasting memorial to the man, no matter how anonymous he was on the vast battlefields of World War II; they are a reminder that he lived, and that eventually he died before his time. It is

important that we regard these cards with decent respect, no matter what our beliefs, as tangible evidence of the cost of war, which usually robs a generation of its youngest, healthiest and bravest. Think about them as they look back at you from these pages; once, they were very like you and me.

(**Left & above**) Rare images of a funeral for Panzer soldiers somewhere on the Eastern Front, with an honour guard firing party dressed in black *Panzerdienstanzug*.

Unteroffizier Sebastian Gröschl

The 26-year-old Sebastian Gröschl was the tank gunner in a PzKw VI Tiger commanded by Leutnant Hans Bölter, a Knight's Cross holder who served with schwere Panzer Abteilung 502 on the northern sector of the Russian Front, operating in summer 1944 in the Kurland Peninsula on the Baltic coast.

On the morning of 13 August 1944 their Tiger was about to commence an attack when they received a call to go to the aid of another tank immobilized by battery problems. Leaving safe cover, Bölter's tank was crossing a field when it suddenly came under fire from its front left. An anti-tank shell penetrated just behind the driver's hull position and passed diagonally back into the fighting compartment, instantly killing both the loader, Richter, and the gunner, Sebastian Gröschl. The tank immediately caught fire, probably by the ignition of spilled propellant from smashed-open shells in the ready use racks – by far the most frequent cause of the catastrophic destruction of tanks in combat. While trying to bale out Bach, the radio operator/hull machine gunner, was shot and killed; only the driver and Leutnant Bölter escaped, both of them severely wounded.

Once the action was over the bodies of Gröschl, Richter and Bach were buried in a local military cemetery. Unteroffizier Gröschl now lies in the German war cemetery at Saldus, Latvia, in Block X, Row 19, Grave 800.

This remembrance set is interesting because it contains not only the card, but also a postcard photograph (in which Gröschl can be seen to wear a civilian checked shirt), and the enamel gravestone ornament made from this image. The back of the postcard photo gives not only his date of death, but also the stamp of the maker of the plaque, Fritz Krug Porzellan-Fabrik of Lauf bei Nürnberg, and a note that two copies of the plaque have been ordered.

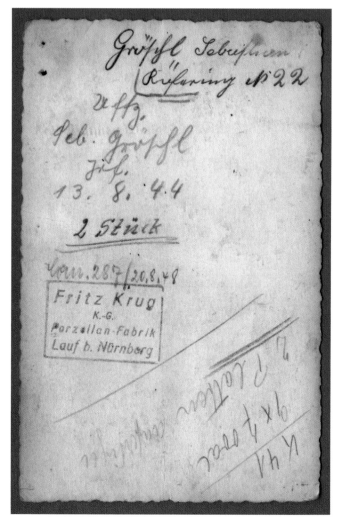

Zum frommen Andenken
für
Franz Leopold
SCHNEEBAUER
Forstwartsohn von Lindertwald
Pfarre St. Florian
Obergefreiter in einem Panzerregiment
Träger des Panzersturmabzeichen
und Inhaber des EK II. Klasse
welcher in Rußland beim Orte Borgowo
im 23. Lebensjahr den Heldentod fand
und im Heldenfriedhof in Rschew
begraben liegt.

Eltern, Geschwister und Freunde mein,
So gern schrieb ich aus der Ferne heim.
Doch heut ist es zum letztenmal
Daß ich Euch grüße tausendmal,
Und sage Dank für jede Gab,
Die ich von Euch empfangen hab.
Richte an Euch die letzte Bitt'
Vergeßt ja im Gebet mich nicht,
Und keine Träne, keine Klag,
Der liebe Gott, der mir das Leben gab
Rief mich so früh ins Heldengrab
Ich werde in des Himmelsauen
Im Lorbeerkranz euch wiederschauen.

(Left) Obergefreiter Franz Schneebauer was just 23 years old when he was killed outside the Russian city of Rzhev, northwest of Moscow, during the first great Soviet winter counter-offensive in January 1942. He was already a holder of the Iron Cross Second Class and the Tank Battle Badge. The back of the card notes that he took part in the invasions of the Low Countries and France, the friendly expeditions to Romania and Bulgaria, and combat in the Balkans. The site of his grave is no longer known.

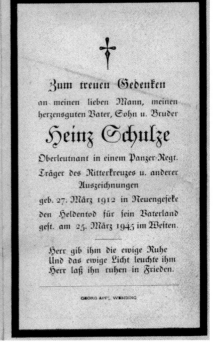

† Zum treuen Gedenken
an meinen lieben Mann, meinen herzensguten Vater, Sohn u. Bruder
Heinz Schulze
Oberleutnant in einem Panzer-Regt.
Träger des Ritterkreuzes u. anderer Auszeichnungen
geb. 27. März 1912 in Neuengeseke
den Heldentod für sein Vaterland
gest. am 25. März 1945 im Westen.

Herr gib ihm die ewige Ruhe
Und das ewige Licht leuchte ihm
Herr laß ihn ruhen in Frieden.

GEORG APP., WENDING

Andenken
an den Obergefreiten

Ludwig Weber
Fahrer bei einer Panzerabteilung
von Neukirchen hl. Blut
geboren am 20. Auguſt 1920
gefallen am 6. März 1943 bei
Medinine (Afrika).

O Eltern und Geſchwiſter mein,
Ich kehre nicht mehr zu Euch heim
Der letzte Gedanke, der letzte Blick
Der eilte noch zu Euch zurück.
Ich weiß, ihr werdet bitter weinen,
Daß ich ſo ferne ſank ins Grab
Wo nur die ſtillen Sterne ſcheinen,
In meine dunkle Gruft hinab.

A. Hœrmann, Neukirchen hl. Blut.

(Left) The 22-year-old tank driver Obergefreiter Ludwig Weber lies today with his comrades in the Bordj-Cedria war cemetery in Tunisia. He died on 6 March 1943 in the battle of Medenine – Rommel's failed last attack on Montgomery's 8th Army, just three days before the 'Desert Fox' left Africa for the last time. Weber probably perished in one of the 50-plus Panzers lost, out of about 145 – from 10., 15. & 21. Panzer Divisions – which took part in the attack.

(Above) Oberleutnant Heinz Schulze was a holder of the Knight's Cross. The commander of a Panther tank with the highly regarded 116. Panzer Division, he was killed on 25 March 1945 – just two days before his 33rd birthday – while countering a thrust by the US 30th Infantry Division into the Ruhr Pocket. The photo shows him as a Stabsfeldwebel at the time of his award of the *Ritterkreuz* in August 1943; he also displays the Iron Cross, Tank Battle Badge, silver Wound Badge, and a ribbon bar for a Long Service medal and another unidentified award.

Select bibliography

Ailsby, Christopher, *Combat Medals of the Third Reich*, Patrick Stephens Ltd (Northamptonshire, UK, 1987)

Angolia, John R., *For Führer and Fatherland – Military Awards of the Third Reich*, Vol 1, R.James Bender Publishing Co. (San Jose, CA, USA, 1976)

Angolia, John R. & Schlicht, Adolf, *Uniforms & Traditions of the German Army*, 3 vols, R.James Bender Publishing Co. (San Jose, CA, USA, 1984)

Bender, Roger J. & Odegard, Warren W., *Uniforms, Organization and History of the Panzertruppe*, R.James Bender Publishing Co. (San Jose, CA, USA, 1980)

Ehrich, Dr. Curt, *Uniformen und Soldaten*, Erich Klinghammer Verlag (Berlin, Germany, 1942)

Forty, George, *German Tanks of World War II*, Arms & Armour Press (London, UK, 2000)

Heukemes, Frank, *German Awards of World War II – The General Assault Badge*, Heukemes Publishing (Germany, 2005)

Hormann, Jörg M., *Uniforms of the Panzer Troops 1917 to the Present*, Schiffer Publishing (PA, USA, 1989)

Krawczyk, Wade, *Army Panzer Uniforms in Colour Photographs*, Crowood Press (Wiltshire, UK, 1999)

Kurowski, Franz, *Die Tiger Kommen!*, Podzun-Pallas Verlag (Wölfersheim-Berstadt, Germany, 2001)

Mitcham, Samuel W., *Hitler's Legions – German Army Order of Battle World War II*, Leo Cooper with Secker & Warburg Ltd (London, UK, 1985)

Pruett, Michael H., & Edwards, Robert J., *Field Uniforms of German Army Panzer Forces in World War II*, J.J.Fedorowicz Publishing Inc. (Winnipeg, Canada, 1993)

Pruett, Michael H., & Edwards, Robert J., *Field Uniforms of Germany's Panzer Elite*, J.J.Fedorowicz Publishing Inc. (Winnipeg, Canada, 1998)

Rebentisch, Ernst, *Zum Kaukasus und zu den Tauern – Die Geschichte der 23. Panzer Division*, self-published on behalf of the veteran members of the 23. Pz Div (Stuttgart, Germany, 1963)

Sánchez, Alfonso Escuadra, *Feldherrnhalle: Forgotten Elite*, Shelf Books (West Yorkshire, UK, 1996)

Wegmann, Günter, *Die Ritterkreuzträger der Panzertruppe*, Band 1, Biblio Verlag (Bissendorf, Germany, 2004)

Westarp, E.-J. Graf von, *Taschenkalender für Offiziere des Heeres*, Alfred Waberg Verlag (Pommern, Germany, 1943)